AVANTI POPOLO

Italian-American Writers Sail Beyond Columbus

edited by
The Italian-American Political Solidarity Club

Manic D Press
San Francisco

Thanks to the people and venues who have hosted Avanti Popolo readings: Peter Maravelis/City Lights, Father Louis Vitale/Saint Boniface Church, Amanda Davidson/Modern Times, and Josie's Juice Joint and Cabaret. Thanks also to Maria Lisella and Gil Fagiani for making "above and beyond" their standard operating procedure.

Front cover photo: 1927 protest against the execution of Nicola Sacco and Bartolomeo Vanzetti
Front cover image / Columbus landing: Dutch, 16th century
Back cover photo / Columbus statue: ©iirraa

Cataloging-in-Publication Data is on file with the Library of Congress.

For our friend

Guiliana Milanese

a fantastic union organizer
teaching generations of Italian-American organizers
that pride in our community
can only be earned through our solidarity with others

Contents

AVANTI

SAILING BEYOND COLUMBUS

Historically, Italian Americans adopted Columbus as their hero for an obvious reason: We needed to feel validated in a land where we were not accepted. When we arrived here in huge numbers in the late 1800s fleeing terrible poverty (which unification of Italy in 1861 only exacerbated), we weren't exactly greeted with open arms. In fact, there were "No Italians Need Apply" notices in shop windows, lynchings in the South, and a widely held belief that we were going to bring down Anglo-Saxon culture with our barbaric Latin ways.

While the Mafia may have once driven foreign invaders from parts of southern Italy, it became a crime organization that terrorized the lives of the very people it once defended. But the gun-toting "La cosa nostra" families weren't the most feared: it was the southern Italian anarchists and labor organizers that the government went after with a vengeance in the early 1900s. Two of them, Nicola Sacco and Bartolomeo Vanzetti, were falsely accused of murdering two bank payroll clerks. During their trial, the judge referred to them as "dagos," a derogatory term for Italians. Despite worldwide protests and the support of prominent figures including Upton Sinclair, Sacco and Vanzetti were executed in 1927.

During WWII, thousands of Italian immigrants were forcibly relocated from their homes or tossed into jail under suspicion of being enemy aliens, losing their livelihoods while their sons fought overseas on behalf of the U.S. In Little Italys, signs cautioned residents not to speak "the enemy tongue," which discouraged parents from passing on their language to their children.

In the '60s, a new image emerged of Italian Americans as conservative and racist. In Philadelphia, an Italian American named Frank Rizzo made a national reputation for himself as a tough cop turned even tougher Police Commissioner. "Spacco il capo, (split their heads)" was his slogan. He humiliated the Black Panthers by having them strip-searched outside their headquarters in front of the press. He stopped drag queens from parading on Halloween night. He sent tanks to prevent anti-war marchers from reaching City Hall on the day after Kent

State. When he was elected mayor, he broke the glass ceiling for Italian American politicians in that East Coast city but he became a right-wing stereotype that haunts us still.

Few remember Harlem Congress member Vito Marcantonio, a champion for the people and a strong civil rights advocate. A card-carrying member of the American Labor Party, he built an historic coalition among Italians, Puerto Ricans, African Americans, and poor whites in his district. When faced with defeat after fourteen years in Congress, Marcantonio told Congress: "I have not retreated, I do not apologize, and I am not compromising."

This is the Italian American tradition with which we identify. When our government tries to punish those from south of the border who come here to work by any means necessary, we Italian Americans need to be in the streets with them to say "Hell No!" When workers are mistreated or paid wages they cannot live on, we Italian Americans need to be there to fight for a living wage for all, as our predecessors did.

In San Francisco, the Italian American Political Solidarity Club, composed solely of poets and writers of Italian ancestry, initiated an annual October 12th reading entitled "Dumping Columbus" to celebrate the radical traditions of our southern Italian paesani/e. This book was inspired by these annual celebrations. It's essential for us to take a stand, reclaiming and remembering our heritage.

There may be some who will accuse us of hating our own people for raising our voices in support of those under the boot of oppression today. We consider it to be the highest form of love, not just for our own people, but for all of humanity. Whether it be universal healthcare or gay rights, affordable housing or an end to war, we Italian Americans need to lift our collective voices for social and economic justice for all once again.

It's time.

Tommi Avicolli Mecca

A FEW REASONS TO SAIL BEYOND COLUMBUS

Many people who share our Italian-American heritage have accomplishments we can embrace. Cristoforo Colombo, who kicked off a legacy of slavery, brutality and war, should not be celebrated as a hero when there are so many others deserving of our respect. By breaking with the Columbus myth, we honor—not dishonor—our heritage.

Slavery and Brutality

In 1492, slavery existed in various forms throughout the world. However, it was Columbus who started the Atlantic slave trade. Columbus shipped about 5,000 Indian slaves to Spain. In 1505, his son started trafficking African slaves to the New World.

On his second voyage, Columbus initiated war to conquer the Indians. In 1492, the Arawak tribe had little in the way of weapons to defend themselves. In addition to unleashing European weapons (cannon, lances, swords, etc.) he brought hunting dogs to kill Indians.

Life under Spanish rule in the new world was brutal from the beginning. Columbus required Indians to pay tribute of gold dust to Catholic overseers. Upon paying the tax, Indians received a token to wear to prove the payment had been made. Those with expired tokens had their hands cut off.

Columbus began the "encomienda" system that stole native villages and awarded them to colonists. The slavery that followed drove many natives to suicide.

He Didn't "Discover" Anything...

We are taught that Columbus discovered a new world. Fact is that many thousands of tribes were already here! These tribes, called "Indians," populated the continent from the southernmost tip of Argentina to the northernmost point of Canada.

There is considerable evidence that many previous explorers may have reached the Americas from Japan, Indonesia, West African and Greenland.

Genocide

Within four years of Columbus's arrival, his men had killed or exported one-third of the original Indian population.

Racism

In order to justify the conquest, a system of racist classifications became necessary. These systems not only deprive conquered people of livelihoods, resources and freedom, they also rob European-Americans of connections to their own vibrant and dynamic cultures (e.g., Italian, Irish, Spanish), instead melding them into a single "white race" which simply did not exist before colonization of the Americas.

By the Way...

Columbus got lost. He was looking for India, but found the "Americas."

His ships were sponsored by Spain, not Italy. Italy didn't even exist as a unified, single country at the time.

In 1492, many other navigators believed the world was round, not flat.

Source:
James Loewen, "Lies My Teacher Told Me About Christopher Columbus," The New Press, 1992.

AVANTI

Forward!

WHOSE DAY IS IT ANYWAY?
Diane di Prima
The Poet Mulls over Some of the Choices

Pola Negri Day?
Joe DiMaggio Day?
Sacco and Vanzetti Day!

Lawrence Ferlinghetti Day?
Tina Modotti Day?
Sacco and Vanzetti Day!

Carlo Tresca Day?
Gregory Corso Day?
Sacco and Vanzetti Day!

Tony Bennett Day!
Phil Rizzuto Day
Sacco and Vanzetti Day!

Domenico Mallozzi Day!
Sal Maglie Day
Sacco and Vanzetti Day!

Al Pacino Day.
Frank Sinatra Day.
Sacco and Vanzetti Day!

Francis Coppola Day.
Chick Correa Day.
Sacco and Vanzetti Day!

Robert Di Niro Day
Guy Lombardo Day
Sacco and Vanzetti Day.

Joseph Stella Day
Frank Stella Day

Philip Lamantia Day
Tina Modotti Day

Frankie Laine Day
Mario Lanza Day
Riker's Island Day

Joe Pesci
Brian De Palma
Sacco and Vanzetti Day

Frank Capra of Happy Endings & Leftist Leanings Day!
That's one we could use.

Il Giorno di Leslie Scalapino!
Il Giorno di Ben Gazzara!
Il Giorno di Sacco e Vanzetti!

Il Giorno di Martino Scorsese.
Il Giorno di Tomaso Centalella
Tutti giorni sono giorni di Sacco e Vanzetti

Is it your day, Rocky Graziano,
idol of my teen years
with your thick voice on the radio
        "It was a good fight
        I was in good condition
        Hello, Ma"
(I got your autograph at a grocery store on Spring St)

Madonna?
Madonna Mia or as we used to say
"Marron!"

Back in the Day
It was Connie Francis Day

Then a few years later it was
Julie Bovasso Day
Julie doing "The Maids"
in a tiny downtown theatre,
turning gender & theatre around / 1952

Whose day is it anyway?
Maybe we could rename it
every year–

Then maybe today would be
Tony La Russa Day?
        Carpe Diem, Tony!
You never know, you know?

Joe Montana
Maria Mazziotti Gillan
Phil Cavaretta
Ani Di Franco
Vick Damone
Jimmy Giuffre
Whose Day is it?
Alan Alda
Joe Lovano

Judy Canova Day
Her loud voice on the big wooden radio

Jimmy Durante
        "Good night, Mrs. Calabash–
        (or whatever that name was he said
        week after week
        I never figured it out–)

Goodnight, Mrs. Calabash
   wherever you are"
And the grown-ups would turn off the radio
and we'd go to bed.

O It's Louis Prima Day, for sure!
We gotta have one of those!
Or wait

Who knew it could be
Frank Zappa Day
Was he actually born on this planet?

Aha! I've got it—
Yogi Berra Day
Yogi Berra Day

Yogi Berra Day
Tina Modotti Day

Yogi Berra Day
Sacco and Vanzetti Day
Yogi Berra Day

Sacco and Vanzetti Day
Yogi Berra Day
Sacco and Vanzetti Day

You choose

THE LIGURIAN
Tad Tuleja

Genoa's boy. Your name flowers from the sea
You conquered to the one you never saw
From the country of the Caribs to Sacagawea's, you are still
The first American dreamer—he who tore the curtain,
Exploding the world.

But when I dream of you, Ligurian, I don't see the admiral
Or the reckless explorer, calming his
Terrified crew. I don't see the reverent captain
Planting the green cross, looking at the dark eyes
Looking at him.

When I dream of you, Ligurian, I see virgin land.
Green parrots. Pure beaches. And naked people
Bringing fruit and flowers. Cutting themselves on your steel,
They wonder if you bleed red. Someone says "Save us."
Nobody breathes.

When I dream of you, Ligurian, I see a child on the docks.
He watches the old sea dogs. He listens to the chattering sails,
The mysterious dialects. How lucky you were, little Christopher,
When the only gold you desired glinted
In the eye of heaven.

TOTALITARIAN DEMOCRACY
Lawrence Ferlinghetti

The first fine dawn of life on earth
The first light of the first morning
The first evening star
The first man on the moon seen from afar
The first voyage of Ulysses westward
The first fence on the last frontier
The first tick of the atomic clock of fear
The first Home Sweet Home so dear
The sweet smell of honeysuckle at midnight
The first free black man free of fright
The sweet taste of freedom
The first good orgasm
The first Noble Savage
The first Pale Face settler on the first frontier
The last Armenian and the last Ojibway in Fresno
The first ballpark hotdog with mustard
The first home run in Yankee Stadium
The first song of love and forty cries of despair
The first pure woman passing fair
The sweet smell of success
The first erection and the first Resurrection
The first darling buds of May
The last covered wagon through the Donner Pass
The first green sprouts of new grass
The last cry of Mark Twain! on the Mississippi
The First and Last Chance Saloon
The ghostly galleon of the half-moon
The first cry of pure joy in morning light
The distant howl of trains lost in book of night
The first morning after the night before thinking
The last new moon sinking
The last of the Mohicans and the last buffalo

The last sweet chariot swinging low
The first hippie heading for the hills
The last bohemian in a beret
The last beatnik in North Beach with something to say
The last true love to come your way
The last Wobbly and the last Catholic Anarchist
The last paranoid Lefty
The last Nazi
The first bought vote in the first election
The last hand caught in the last cookie jar
The last cowboy on the last frontier
The last bald eagle with nothing to fear
The last buffalo head nickel
The last living member of the Abraham Lincoln Brigade
The last Mom and Pop grocery
The last firefly flickering in the night

The first plane to hit the first Twin Tower
The last plane to hit the last Twin Tower
The only plane to ever hit the Pentagon
The birth of a vast national paranoia
The beginning of the Third World War
(the War Against the Third World)

The first trip abroad by an ignorant president
The last free-running river
The last gas and oil on earth
The last general strike
The last Fidelista the last Sandinista the last Zapatista
The last political prisoner
The last virgin and the last of the champagne
The last train to leave the station
The last and only great nation
The last Great Depression
The last will & testament
The last welfare check for rent

The end of the old New Deal
The new Committee on Unamerican Activities
The last politician with honest proclivities
The last independent newspaper
printing the news and raising hell
The last word and the last laugh and the Last Hurrah
The last picture show and the last waltz
The last Unknown Soldier
The last innocent American
The last Ugly American
The last Great Lover and the last New Yorker
The last home-fries with ketchup-to-go
The last train home at midnight
The last syllable of recorded time
The last long careless rapture
The last independent bookstore with its own mind
The last best hope of mankind
The lost chord and the lost leader
The last drop of likker
The cup that runneth over quicker
The last time I saw Paris Texas
The last peace treaty and the Last Supper
The first sweet signs of spring
The first sweet bird of youth
The first baby tooth and the last wisdom tooth
The last honest election
The last freedom of information
The last free Internet
The last free speech radio
The last unbought television network
The last homespun politician
The last Jeffersonian
The last Luddite in Berkeley
The last Bottom Line and the last of Social Security
The first fine evening calm and free
The beach at sunset with reclining nudes

the lovers wrapped in each other
The last meeting of the Board
The last gay sailor to come aboard
The first White Paper written in blood
The last terrorist born of hate and poverty
The last citizen who bothered to vote
The first President picked by a Supreme Court
The end of the Time of Useful Consciousness
The unfinished flag of the United States
The ocean's long withdrawing roar

The birth of a nation of sheep
The deep deep sleep of the booboisie
The underground wave of feel-good fascism
The uneasy rule of the super-rich
The total triumph of imperial America
The final proof of our Manifest Destiny
The first loud cry of America über alles
Echoing in freedom's alleys
The last lament for lost democracy
The total triumph of
totalitarian plutocracy

CODA

Cut down cut down cut down
Cut down the grassroots
Cut down those too wild weeds
in our great agri-fields and golf courses
Cut down cut down those wild sprouts
Cut down cut down those rank weeds
Pull down your vanity, man, pull down
the too wild buds the too wild shoots
Cut down the wild unruly vines & voices
the hardy volunteers and pioneers
Cut down cut down the alien corn

Cut down the crazy introverts
Tongue-tied lovers of the subjective
Cut down cut down the wild ones the wild spirits
The desert rats and monkey wrenchers
Easy riders and midnight cowboys in narco nirvanas
Cut down the wild alienated loners
fiddling with their moustaches
plotting revolution in hopeless cellars
Cut down cut down all those freaks and free thinkers
Wild-eyed poets with wandering minds
Soapbox agitators and curbstone philosophers
Far out weirdos and rappers
Stoned-out visionaries and peaceniks
Exiles in their own land!
O melting pot America!

LEGACY
Rosemary Petracca Cappello

My father's father, Antonio Petracca, came to this country
alone, leaving his wife and son in Teano, Italy.
His five other children died in infancy or childhood.

Antonio settled in Ardmore, Pennsylvania and worked
for wealthy homeowners on the Main Line. He was a
prize-winning gardener by summer; by winter, he tended
furnaces. He died before I was born. My knowledge of him
is in a photograph taken in the shadow of the foliage he grew.

In 1916, Antonio sent for his son, Giovanni, my father,
born in 1900, not wanting him to die in World War I.

My grandmother, Giuseppa Conte, also known as Giuseppina
or Pippinella, made the trip here with Giovanni. Their boat
docked in Boston where they saw snow for the first time.
Giuseppina thought it was the end of the world. From there,
they traveled to their new home on Cricket Avenue in Ardmore.

Giovanni was a skilled shoemaker, having learned his craft
as a boy from his uncle Antonio Conte. Here, Antonio Petracca
set him up with shops in three locations: Ardmore, Oakmont,
and Llanerch. Antonio died in 1927, so didn't see his son
lose his shops in the Great Depression.

My mother's father, Geremia Arcaro, came here from
Campobasso. He had a grocery store in front of his house
at 520 West Butler Street in a northern section of Philadelphia.

He married Filomena Tamburri, also from Campobasso,
who bore him 14 children (six died in infancy) and helped
him in the store. Every morning, at the earliest of hours,

she went to the docks, selecting the freshest produce for sale,
some of which she pickled or canned and sold as preserves.

My mother, Rose Arcaro, called Rosina by my father,
was born in Philadelphia in 1903. Twelve years old when
her mother died, she raised her four younger siblings.
It was she who told me the facts, here, that I wouldn't
otherwise have known. My father died in 1974;
my mother, in 1984.

All of those named here left a legacy of Hard Work and Silence.
I embrace the work; reject the silence.

ORANGE ALERT CREEPING INTO RED
Thomas Centolella

What I wanted was a brain, a heart, and courage,
and what I got was the shock and awe
of a dumbass fumbling behind the curtain
of imminent threat. I wanted to bring back Harold Arlen
to teach inspiration at the University of the Genuine,
and I wanted an all-natural, non-synthesized,
cost effective, readily available, and gleefully affordable
anodyne for all optimists undermined by manic depression.
What I got was a Yemeni in short sleeves and khakis
sitting on the sidewalk with a pepperoni slice,
flanked by two sturdy suitcases, one of them
yellow as the taxi from the airport there's no way he could afford.
I wanted the peace that passeth all understanding, and what I got
was an axis of evil, tax cuts for the entitled, susceptible levees,
and the stunning tenth-grader waiting for a streetcar named For Hire
who when asked where she was going replied, "An appointment,"
the look from her mascara'd eyes too knowing. I wanted alliances
and allegiances, and what I got was a suspicion of pathogens
simmering in the Yemeni's Samsonite. What I got was an old Paiute
at the free clinic who said, "Stay calm. Be brave. Wait for signs."
OK, Chief. And if the signs don't come? "Then that's a sign."

LATEST NEWS
Al Tacconelli

To fight for freedom's illusion, more troops needed.
For an absurdity more men and women will risk lives
where life is cheap and death comes easy.

Blood soaked desert sands are pathetic memorials.
War's only victory is death; the more killed,
the more victorious, and the rest —
relentless, thought robbing propaganda.

Bring home our troops — to live long lives
surrounded by loved ones. Let those who shout,
"Destroy The Terrorists," don camouflaged uniforms,
how quickly then the fiasco would end.

THE FIGHT
Cameron McHenry

I was innocent once, and believed that the world was just;
evil acts and unruly children were sent to the corner
to learn their lesson:

"Bad kid! Go to the corner to pay penance
 for the wrong you've inflicted."

Children pushed their pissy faces into the sharp angles of solitude
and quickly learned that time-out was no fun.

Just the same, one summer when no one was looking,
Julie Jones dropped a giant rock on my bare foot.
She did it because I would give her anything,
because she was older and bigger and could.

My father, a giant ranger and a man of the land,
took me into the backyard
to explain that Julie Jones was like Christopher Columbus.

"Punch my hand as hard as you can," he said,
"punch it because you must learn to fight for goodness."

I was horrified. Where was the corner for her to stand in—
all the strict lines enforcing right and wrong?

"Right here," my father said, slipping his fist into a ball, stressing
the sharp angle of his wrist bone to the unyielding knob of his elbow,
"this is your edge."

I remained horrified.
Christopher Columbus was a hero and Julie Jones was my best friend.
What the hell was he talking about?

As I grew older, I began to disregard textbook caricatures
and learned that heroism, bravery and faith
also meant conquest, exploitation and slavery,
depending on who was telling the story.

Christopher Columbus was no more an example of:
"monumental feats accomplished through perseverance and faith"
(as quoted by George Bush Senior) than Julie Jones was a nice girl
and worthy friend.

It all made sense the day a tiny Chinese man stepped
in front of a tank—
a common-man hero who threw his precious life before a juggernaut
to light up the globe in an instant.
Seventeen tanks were thrown into the corner
by the 206 unwavering bones
in a single individual's body.

It was a historical time out,
which forced me back into the streets of my neighborhood
to again stand before Julie Jones
—tormenter of every poor kid in town—
and, as demonstrated by my father years before,
I rolled my fist into a symbol of resistance,
and broke that bitch's nose.

There have been since time immemorial
rocks dropped, ships landing and tanks
rolling onto, into and over those
who look up admiringly, swim out excitedly and stand by remorsefully.

In the name of preserving what innocence we can,
I'm choosing to stand next to my father in the back yard,
next to the people whose kindness is at stake,
next to the man in front of the tank

until Christopher, George and Julie Colombo turn the fuck around
and shove their pissy, busted noses back into the corner
to finally learn their lesson.

MY GHOSTS/ i miei fantasmi
Tommi Avicolli Mecca

Vito Marcantonio, I saw you
giving the finger to Congress
as the sons and daughters
of immigrants debated whether a wall
should be built to keep out the huddled masses
yearning to make a decent living

Virgilia d'Andrea, I passed you
on Market Street arguing with that man
holding the blown-up color photo
of an aborted fetus
you were trying to explain that "pro-life"
meant "abbasso il militarismo"

Carlo Tresca, I noticed you on
Haight Street again last night
handing out literature to the
skater boys and the fake dreadlock girls
you were telling them about the rising proletariat
but their headphones were too loud

Maria Barbieri, you came back
to an America where there were no more
Italian women working in sweatshops but
a trip to China made you weep
for the millions on endless assembly lines
assembling things non vale niente

Ferndinando Nicola Sacco and Bartolomeo Vanzetti
I glimpsed you carrying those hot meals
in brown paper bags to AIDS patients
living in a hospice in the Castro

from the way you two were arguing
I thought you were an old couple

Angela Bambace, Albina Delfino, Tina Catania
Antonetta Lazzaro, Tina Gaeta, Margaret diMaggio
Lucia Romualdi, tutte donne sovversive
you are in every street in which I march
every rally I attend
you are not silent ghosts

(abbasso il militarismo: "down with militarism"
tutte donne sovversive: "all subversive women"
non vale niente: "not worth anything, worthless")

FROM THE LIFE OF A CIRINO
Leonard Cirino

after Joao Cabral de Melo Neto as translated by Elizabeth Bishop

Leonard is a lion. Cirino means
match, or quick to light.
My father's bad temper was brought to me
by birth. I've stewed in that broth for years.

My youth was more like a hyena,
laughing and hungry. My age has brought
an elephant plagued with memories
I'll take to the grave.

My ancestors grew grapes
on the scrappy land near Naples.
They watered the soil with tears
to keep their roots strong.

One woman called my brother, a peasant
intellectual so I've taken it for myself.
I've sown and am sewn together
with ideas from many sources.

I pick and choose, then steal
the very best baubles for my own.
Not greedy, here I am
sharing them with you.

Not too deep, unlike rich soil.
the intermittent stones and leached land
are more like what I cultivate,
from which come grapes, and hence, wine.

Grandfather emigrated in 1910.
He grew tomatoes for sauce, not grapes.

The grapes he bought at market
to make the red wine he drank everyday.

Grandmother made the sauce for spaghetti,
raviolis. It took her two days to get it just so.
She'd simmer, stir, and skim just the right
amount of tomatoes, sausage, spices.

Lots of basil and garlic, no oregano.
She attended church every day,
as well as her sons whom she doted over,
and her daughters who both finished college.

She never let anyone, not even her husband,
kiss her on the lips. She said, These lips
are saved for Jesus, and, at 101, she got
her wish and flew to heaven.

My Uncle Nick was an architect
and an engineer. He designed
the first skyscrapers in LA, called
the Tishman Buildings.

He also tried to get housing for the poor
at Chavez Ravine before the Dodgers.
When the city fathers sold out to the
baseball powers he knew his first defeat.

Called in front of the HUAC for criticizing
the decision, the newspaper photo showed him
shaking his finger at McCarthy. The caption
said he told McCarthy to go to hell.

When I was twelve he gave me
the Cannery Row series. Very early
I learned my politics and love

of literature from him.

That's enough for now. Remember,
I'm old now but still a bull elephant.
I love and hate with equal passion,
live on the edge, with both shoulders sloped.

IF COLUMBUS DISCOVERED AMERICA THEN...
James Tracy

Bombay is home to many Tainos
Matthew Shepard discovered Colorado
Elvis invented Rock and Roll
Queen Isabella ruled Italy
Fat Man discovered Nagasaki

(The cockroach discovered the sandwich)

The bulldozer discovered the tenement
Ruby Rodriguez discovered the Mission District
The earth is only round enough to balance a nightstick on it
Denial is a river in Egypt

 The Panama Canal runs through the North Carolina
El Salvador is India
Little Boy discovered Hiroshima
Your grandmother really did know Sinatra

(Yusef Hawkins discovered Bensonhurst)

IMMIGRANT IN PARADISE: COLUMBUS AND 'MAKING' AMERICA
Lawrence DiStasi

Begin by imagining a scene—of Christopher Columbus on his third voyage. The year is 1498. It is six years since The Admiral of the Ocean Sea ran into the islands of the Caribbean, returned in triumph to dazzle Spain and Europe with tales of his "Indios," and attempted a second voyage to colonize them, with disastrous results for both himself and the indigenous peoples. He has neither found the gold he was sure he would find there, nor have his Indios turned out as he first thought these "natural Christians" would: they have proved quite willing to defend themselves, and quite unwilling to be enslaved, or even work. Since the Spaniards who have shipped out to settle Española (now the Dominican Republic and Haiti) have refused to work either, and show nothing but contempt and loathing for the place, Columbus and his brother Bartolomeo have resorted to draconian measures to try to pacify the island and obtain the payoff the Admiral has continually promised, but not found.

Now this, the third voyage, is designed to take the search farther south—to find the passage to India Columbus is sure exists, and to find the wealth he is even surer dwells in the South: the land and/or islands of the antipodes where everything runs counter to the quotidian world of Europe, where headless men walk upside down, and Amazons rule, and gold is not scarce but plentiful as grass. His hope is that this will be a third voyage in every sense of that magical, trinitarian number.

Imagine him where he is, then: having successfully crossed the Atlantic Ocean for the third time, he has sighted Trinidad, the island off the coast of Venezuela, and named it after the holy Trinity. He has navigated the strait between Trinidad and what he takes to be yet another large island but is really the huge South American continent, to enter what appears to be more ocean but is really an enclosed gulf, the Gulf of Paria, formed by Trinidad and the continent. He has sailed north in this Gulf forty miles or so to another narrow exit from this strange sea, a sea where salty ocean water mixes with what seems a miraculous quantity of fresh water. He doesn't attempt to brave this exit yet, though.

He decides to go south, coasting southwest in this tropical, balmy wonderland, as gorgeous a place as he has ever seen or even dreamed of, with palm trees and exotic fruit and natives dressed strangely, and strangely light-skinned—lighter-skinned are these southern Indios, he says, than those in Española, lighter-skinned, too, than the natives of Africa who live at the same parallel, where the searing African heat contrasts remarkably with the balmy climate here. He heads southwest to search out a western exit, the strait that he is sure will take him around what must be a southern island off Asia, and to fabulous India and the lands to its south where he is sure there exists, again parallel with Africa, wealth undreamed of.

The Admiral is not without anxiety about all this. He is carrying three shiploads of supplies for his brother, desperate for them on Española. He is worried about this strange fresh-water sea he's in—a sea he has now christened the Golfo de la Ballena—the gulf of the whale. And the name, as Columbus's names always are, is prophetic, mythic. He is Jonah in the belly of the whale, Columbus is now, and he knows it. He has entered it via a dangerous strait—he names it the Boca de la Sierpe, the mouth of the serpent—which, shortly after it is entered, has struck him with a tidal wave so violent and terrifying that years later he could still, he wrote, "feel that fear in my body lest the ship be swamped when she came beneath it." And while he has found a northern exit, it too smells dangerous because it marks a meeting of two conflicting waters—the ocean trying to enter and the fresh water trying to exit—and so he again mythically names this one the Boca del Dragon: the mouth of the Dragon.

For Columbus, the moment is strange, even dizzying, for he had the habit, when at sea in a new place, of staying awake almost constantly, for weeks at a time. On this voyage, his absolute fascination with the North Star has kept him even more wide-eyed and wild-eyed than usual. By sighting on Polaris at nightfall, at midnight, and at dawn, a 15th century mariner could derive some sense of his latitude. Longitude was a matter for instinct alone, but latitude Columbus could determine by the reading at nightfall. It was in this way that he had concluded he was at about the latitude of Sierra Leone in Africa, near the equator. The trouble was, he was also finding a huge disparity between the reading of his star at nightfall and at dawn—some ten degrees—which meant to him something very strange indeed. It meant he had entered a new zone. A special zone, a literally higher zone, though he wouldn't make sense of it until later.

Then he got the news from a ship he had sent to reconnoiter: the exit at the bottom of the gulf (the South American continent itself), which he was sure was the strait to India, turned out to be, appeared to be—a river! Several river mouths. Huge. Unprecedented in their hugeness. A monstrous flow of fresh water was entering the Whale Gulf, so it had to be a river (it was in fact the Orinoco, part of the Amazon). But at first the Admiral refused to believe it. So much water was unheard of, not even the Nile or the Ganges produced such volume. And Columbus was insightful enough as a geographer to realize what it meant: such a huge river would require not a mere island, but the drainage from a huge land mass, a whole continent. Or a miracle.

Confusion. It was all so confusing and he was so exhausted and pressed for time. And then there were the natives. His men had gone ashore. The natives welcomed them in their 'naturally Christian', beautiful way. Fed them, feasted them, made love with them, gave them chicha—the maize liquor of the Indians; in short, treated them like gods and begged them to stay. Promised that there was much gold over the hills (though frustratingly, the metal they actually possessed was a mixture of gold and copper—guanin they called it—and useless from Columbus's point of view.) Showed them pearls, enormous quantities of pearls which, the natives indicated, could be had by the bushel on the ocean side.

Pearls. The pearl of great price. It was not exactly what he had been hoping for, praying for. It was not the strait or the gold (though in fact there would later turn out to be Andean gold and silver in quantities that even Columbus would have found miraculous). But it was something. And that something, all these various somethings breaking over him like that monstrous tidal wave, breaks him.

Or rather, something in Columbus breaks here. Something breaks. The tension of not knowing, of not finding what the monarchs have been pressuring him so to find, and of now being lost, trapped in dangerous shoaling waters that make no sense, land that makes no sense, climate that makes no sense, his hopes once again dashed, his beliefs once again hard up against intractable, damnable facts—something breaks. He cannot muscle the new world here as he has elsewhere, as he had on the second voyage when he had forced his crew to swear that Cuba was not an island as everything indicated, but a mainland. No, he cannot. And so the new world breaks in upon him, and he knows, though he will to the end of his days deny it, that this new world is, in fact, a new world. Another orb entirely, an otro mundo, he calls it in his letter to the Spanish monarchs, and it is paradisal. In fact, this is as close as Columbus ever gets to a real, an authentic paradise, which in some part of himself he knows. Knows he has come to the end, has completed his quest, completed himself, and should simply stay. He should stay here in paradise. Be in paradise. Give in to the immobility, which to him is paralysis, of Paradise.

And yet. He does not. That also breaks. He does not stay because he cannot; he has to get moving again, he knows, or die, the whole Indies project will die. So he orders his men to return to the ship, leave the women (save for four Indians he orders seized as "specimens"), leave the chicha, leave the heavenly feel of being treated as gods, and be ready to sail at midnight. And he does. He sails north to the Boca del Dragon, stalls terrified by the clash of waters and winds unable to go back or forward or move at all—until somehow, at the most perilous, paralyzed moment, when all three ships are about to be cast upon the rocks by the currents, feels himself miraculously popped out of the strait, out of the belly of the whale through the mouth of the dragon he is popped like a baby birthed from the womb, "without a scratch."

Thus reborn, the Admiral exults in the movement of sail and wind, of being on the move, always happier Columbus was to be on the ocean and so in motion right past the pearls he directs all three ships as if afraid to stop, hoping he can retrieve them on another trip but never doing so at all. Others harvested his precious pearls, and the non-sailor Vespucci, the very next year, embarked on the voyage that had his name affixed to the entire land mass Columbus had found. But never mind, without a pause, he heads securely north in what will become his greatest feat of dead reckoning ever, hitting from a strange longitude the island of Española within a few miles of where he has aimed himself.

Which wasn't even the most important thing. More important is what happens on the way. Moving, he is at last moving. And looking back to where he has been. And looking back, he is writing about it in his journal, and meditating on the strangeness he has just witnessed—the North Star variations, and the temperate climate, and the paradisal place its people called 'Paria,' 'Paria'—*Paraiso*—that's it! Where he has just been is, it must have been: Paradise. The Earthly Paradise. For do not all the holy books say the Earthly Paradise stands at the farthest point in the East, that it is temperate, that there is a huge outpouring of waters which makes it the source of all the great rivers? They do. Which must be where that huge volume of fresh water was coming from, the heights of Paradise, and that's where I was, writes Columbus looking backwards. I have been near Paradise.

Now. Most commentators have found this material embarrassing. Columbus really lost it here, they say. These mad ravings after losing all that sleep must be an aberration in an otherwise great mind, a prototype Renaissance mind that at this moment reverted to naïve medievalism. But in a real sense, a mythopoetic sense, they are wrong. This is the essential Columbus. The rational, that is, rationalizing Columbus. Who cannot simply be, but must think, must do, must make something. For the point is this. Columbus was, in fact, in a kind of paradise. The most paradisal place he had ever been, or ever would be. Or perhaps anyone ever will be: in a world fresh, new, unfettered, unfiltered, unspoiled. He was there. He was invited to stay. He wanted to stay (and his men certainly did). But he did not stay. He could not. Could not just be. Which is what one does in Paradise. Be in and of one's place.

Rather, Columbus had to get moving. He had to move and do something. Make something. He had to make Paradise in his mind. He had to look back, mentally, and decide, 'that's what it was, I have been in Paradise.' Unable to simply be where he was, he had to get away, and then look back and mentally create it, recreate it, write about it. Make an artifact of it. And, in fact, his artifact endures because his evocation of the new world as paradise, as the site of the Earthly Paradise, is the first move in the long western myth we are all still living—that Paradise is in fact possible here on earth. Do-able. Utopia, all our modern utopias stem from Columbus. And the attempt to make utopias on earth, including socialism, communism, and the American experiment itself (including all its various utopias, like Brook Farm) all stem from this moment. Which is how all the centennials have presented Columbus: as engenderer of the American myth, the paradise-on-earth-can-be-made-by-man myth—to be created first with mental, imaginative moves, then with politico-cultural moves, and more recently with the scientific, technological moves that define our present.

Which is also to say that, Vespucci notwithstanding, it is Columbus who 'makes' America, Columbus who, thereby, creates every Italian immigrant. Consider: In the Italian villages from which most migrants came, a person, no matter how poor or disenfranchised he might be— and most were dirt poor and totally disenfranchised—still had a place. A place to be. As a human, as a Christian, everyone had a being, an identity in place and of place that went back centuries. Of the soil of which they were made. Of the local stone of which their homes were made. Of the village of which their families were made. And knowing this in their bones allowed them to have an identity, a being, regardless of what they did or did not do. Regardless of earthly achievement or possessions, in other words.

When they arrived in America, all that changed, and identity was lost. For them, as for all Europeans, America was the place of no place; the place not of being, but of doing. You are what you do, what you accomplish. It was not enough to simply be a human living, being in place. One had to "make America." This is the expression the Italian immigrants coined, *fare l'America*, and it is a beautiful and multi-leveled expression. It means to "make it" economically, yes, to make money, which is the sign in America always that one has 'done something.' But it also means to make America itself, remake it, make its roads, yes, which is to make its culture, its society, its government, its way of being a paradise. Remake it, retake it out of the wilderness to remake it on the ideal model. Flatten it. Make roads as grids that cut straight through the natural landscape, not circling villages on hilltops according to the natural terrain, as in their native Italy, but flattening the whole thing, including its native people. And in the process, making, remaking oneself, flattening oneself and one's gestural, expressional self as well as remaking oneself as a flat-out and flattened-out mover, maker, doer, shaker.

And for all this, the pattern laid down by Columbus was the ur-process. Columbus in Paria could not simply be; could not simply be in Paradise, be in his place. He had to flee, move on, and then make paradise, think it, construct it as a mental artifact that would have great resonance in the world he was desperate to move up in, the world of great accomplishments by great men whose names, like those of the great Romans even then being resuscitated by the Italian Renaissance, were remembered. And that is precisely what he did. Once out of Paria and away, he looked back on the information he had, and made sense of it by consulting his books and 'realizing' that the place he had been, higher than normal as the North Star proved, was close to heaven because the earth must have a bulge right there, and the bulge, the pear shape, the nipple on the breast of the globe (all his images of mothers are significant), was the site of the Earthly Paradise and he, Columbus, had been approaching it by a gradual ascent. Had found it. And written about it. He wrote about it in his letter to the Spanish Queen. And writing about it, in his view, made it so.

He could not, in sum, be at home in Paria, in Paradise. He could be only the idea of it, the conjuring it and writing about it looking back.

This is the tragedy of us all, particularly us Americans. We cannot simply be. Cannot simply be in place, because the paradise which is being-in-place is not available in America—the place of no place, as the name itself suggests. Named for Amerigo Vespucci, the word "america," as analyzed by Djelal Kadir in *Columbus and the Ends of the Earth*, parses into several roots from Greek—the negative "a," plus the root, "meri", plus the genitive ending for earth, "ge" (from Amerigo)—all of which scans as "no-place-earth." America: no-place land. And if we look closely at America and the settlement of the North American landscape by European immigrants, we see that, in fact, America has always been interpreted by Europeans, acted upon by Europeans as empty, as lacking, as a land of no-place. As U-topia, which itself scans as no-place. And what this suggests is that Americans from the beginning have never been interested in the place as place. As land. As land having meaning and history and depth, as it did to its indigenous peoples. No, the land and its peoples have interested Americans mainly as obstructions blocking movement across and through it to take from it and them whatever could be taken as fast as it could be taken and sold. Land and people as commodities.

In this, as in all things, Columbus in Paria is the progenitor. For if he had indeed found Paradise, if he had been, if not there, at least within striking distance, why did he not stay? Why could he not stay? Peter Mason, in *Deconstructing America*, offers a clue: "the siren-like hold which the natural world of America exerts on Columbus can be shaken off only by the process of disenchantment, by which Columbus transforms the wealth of natural beauty into a commodity" (p. 170). The enchantment of Paradise requires a disenchantment. Otherwise, we fear, we fall back or regress into paralysis, into nothingness, into the annihilation of all boundaries, all oppositions. And one way to disenchant ourselves from all this is to 'transform the wealth of natural beauty into a commodity.' We destroy the natural topography to mine the earth, we flatten the natural topography to grid it and industrialize it for agriculture, we poison the soil and its variety with a pervasive monoculture, and then we destroy once-bountiful agricultural land to fashion endless, invariant, vacant suburbs.

Making America, in this sense, is making America empty. Void of all that makes for place, makes for a place worth living in, makes it a Geography of Nowhere, as James Kunstler puts it. So while Columbus' journey is, indeed, our enduring myth–that is, that Paradise is actually an achievable thing, here on earth–the irony is that that achievement ultimately, and disastrously becomes the achievement of no-place. Or perhaps this is not ironic at all; perhaps it was implicit in the journey, in the language of that journey from the beginning. Paradise, unlike Utopia, is not something we do or make. It is not no-place. Paradise is precisely place, originally a garden. A place that makes us, keeps us in place, provides us with who we are, maintains us as we are. And it is Columbus who shows us just how perilous-seeming the reality of that can be, how urgent appears the need to flee from it.

LAS ANDEANAS IN ASTORIA
Maria Lisella

They arrive from Ecuador,
Bolivia and Peru, on the sidewalks
in Queens they step
in sneakers without socks,
bowler hats top round
gold-toned faces
hair tied back
in little girl braids
that swivel from side to side
between rounded shoulder blades.

They stuff garbage bags
with glass and plastic bottles
pile them one on top of the
other like shiny blue clouds
billowing out of shopping carts
high above their heads.

Their bodies are silent.
Cartwheels squeak
hi-pitched notes rattle
black squirrels scatter
in black branches above.
As if climbing steep, jagged hills
their fists hold tight
feet dig deep into concrete
directing their valuable cargo.

Built low to the ground
like squat mountain climbers
on sturdy, short legs
here, on Crescent St., Astoria.

If they were back home
at vernal equinox and stood
at *Mita del Mundo,* the equator
they would not cast a shadow.

Three miles outside New York City,
at pre-rush hour dawn, their movements
are hushed, deliberate, too early for
shadows, too early for most people.

Half wear their husbands'
white-collared shirts
or teenagers' cast offs
down to their knees.

If they notice me,
they lift their heads or smile,
a flash of gold peeks from
wide, even mouths.

I whisper *"buenos, "* as I run
to wake my heart, my memory
of the new women
who descend now
from the Andes' volcanoes
to Astoria's alleys trading
soda cans and beer bottles
for nickels and dimes.

"PEZZO DA NOVANTA"
Angelo Zeolla

I.
Pezzo da novanta,
The Guido Poet
Stands before you
Head held high
A bold individual with nothing
To give you but these neighborhood verses
That roll thru this basement cafe
off his tongue with cafone candor
kind of like Cadillacs crawling cautious
in forget about it
funeral processions as hearses
haul off the cadaver of that same
old Zip to Saint Raymond's Cemetery.

You know
the one you so enjoy
eulogizing to
starry-eyed black dress
granddaughters
counting off novenas in
Our Lady of whoever pews
with those trite lines of how
he was a hard-working American
who espoused family values,
who towed the party line,
che s' e' fatt' nu cule quadrate*
who never once asked Big Brother
if he was too good to spare a dime.

Pezzo da novanta,
I had you pegged back and
Forth even before

you came prancing into
The social club
the night of
little Carmine's
First Communion
with your
condescending air,
Six thousand dollar suit,
cinematically coiffed hairdo,
reeking of cheap cologne
and dead presidents wadded over
in that silver money clip you copped
at some jewelry store
way out there in
South Shore,
Staten Island.

And you came traipsing
across the parquet floor
With some of that
good ol' blue eyes elegance,
Half stepping to podium,
Wing tips all aflutter,
Manhandling the microphone
(I must say for about
a millisecond I was impressed.)

Then you cleared
your throat
and started to sputter
The same old
lopsided statistics
'bout how we Dagos
got all the other poor
huddled masses beat,

'bout how we've
lost our gold teeth
and penchant for fig trees
in front gardens,

'bout how
We're model Americans
and maybe some of
that assimilation rag
might rub off on those
Mexicans
that man the stoves
in Crosby Pizzeria.

And while decrying
the negative depictions
Relevant to Tony Soprano
While eloquently extolling
the virtue of visionary explorer,
Giovanni da Verazzano,
Giving us your take
on what a
dim lit dive
the U. S. of A would
Be without the contributions
of the descendants of Ancient Rome,
Regaling us with some
apocalyptic alternate
possibility had Chris
Not come over
and declared
the Native population:
Indians.

Pezzo da novanta,
you're one

Ricordatevi di Roma
shy of sounding
like Mussolini

(Che coglione!)

And then you start the same old story
'bout how it's
all about
climbing the
social ladder
'bout how
Bartolomeo and Nicola
were just
two poor Zips
who were victims
of circumstance,
exclaiming:
If one of their compari
back then had let them know the political score...
but then again to make
a frittata you've got to
break quite a few eggs
after all every wine press
has a few dregs.

Pezzo da Novanta,
The name of your
game is perseverance and
Forming new world habits....

According to you:
Va' fa mocc' with
Bilingual Education,
Because the Nuns
at Saint Anthony's

Never co-opted
lily white Anglo-American
vernacular
For that soil filled
slang
spoken by Siciliani e Salernitani.

Secondo te:
We owe America thanks
for reminding us
 day in
 and day out
that if we kept stepping out of line
there would be a shitload of hell to pay
and look at us
now after the many
trials and tribulations
lynchings and exploitation
self hatred and assimilation
until finally we wised up and
got the 'Mericano
routine down
where we fail to
 connect the dots
Never thinking that
 we were once in the
21st century greenhorn's spot
because you've got to pay
a cover charge
somehow
to enter in this
Studio 54 land of the free.

II.

All I have to say is:

I can't figure out
Why a Godfather watchin'
Pasta and provolone eatin'
Half-ass Ed Sullivan
Introducin' Topo Gigio
Mangled Neapolitan
Dialect speakin'
Mario Lanza
And Frank Sinatra
Listenin'
Who wouldn't know
what The fuck
Caruso Crooned
about even
If his words
were like a Figaro
Chain glistenin'
Off some hairy chested
Cammorista throwin'
His cold
glare up and
Down 'O Vicolo
 scopin'
His comare as she passes
 young hash smokin'
Emcees that freestyle:

Ti sei mai chiesto perché???

Some misogynistic shrink seein'
Multilayered wife cheatin'
Guapp', forever retellin'

his Father's old tales
of how
Beautiful the Ninth Ward was
Before the mulignans
Moved in
and razed whatever
Virgin on the
Half-shell front
yard sculpture
they could find too,
Gets you all in a tizzy
mentre Cristoforo
se la passa lisco
 due to historical
Hypocrite cop out
Context that makes
Everything ethnic
And sarcastically unethical.

After all, it was done under
Universal banner of the
Wondrous seafarin'
Small pox carrier hand
Cuttin'
gold lustin'
Indian enslavin'
heathen
Convertin'
Round world
Maintainin'
Spanish crown
Sailin'
Nina
Pinta
Ma
OOOOOOO Santa Mari'

Nata voda co' sta storia!

If you hear a Zip
Exclaimin'
Mannaggia Colombo!
It isn't so outlandish
Because he was probably
Just your
run of the mill
Genovese
who in
The end would
Have been schived
The fuck out
By those first
McKee Port
coal minin'
Gold tooth grinnin'
Braccianti baresi.

Immigrants and imperialists
Are opposite sides of that
 sentimental scratched up
Penny that lovers find on
First date
Washington Square Park
Strolls amidst
the Chess hustlers that
attempt to sucker
some unsuspectin' stoner
poet into a 15 dollar game
when all he has in his pocket
is the twenty-five cents
he found by the
statue of Garibaldi
where the ghosts

of organ grinders
loiter dejected
by the fact that
the monkey no longer
claps in time to
that street sweep
lonely
night shift melody.

Pezzo da Novanta
You'd say I was takin'
crazy pills
But I'm the type to find
More similarities
Between Cristoforo
And Joe Colombo
Than my immigrant
Great War
Grandfather
Wounded
Decorated
Veteran
Made American citizen
By servin' his time in
Lost generation hell.

I'll play Carlo Tresca
To your Generoso Pope
If it means not
Having to be a part of this
Whole Bella Figura
Farce that would have
Me say that Il settentrione
Is where the beatin' heart of
Italian America gets its rhythm.

Pezzo da Novanta,
Your style is fugazi
Piuttosto tamarro
Ve lo dico Chiaro:
Cazzo me ne fotte
Se c'hai del denaro?

(Eh beh?)

BOXING LESSONS
Ed Coletti

Down in the basement
where the heavy green
plywood ping pong table
completed a ring of sorts
with three walls
my head would ring
sharp like a fight bell
sprung back and forth
emitting sparks of pain as light
as I was skinny as a spider
(my wife calls the kid in a picture)
playing ping pong
all over and around that table
six years after my daddy
(what we don't do to please a daddy)
tied the boxing gloves on me
whenever we had company,
plumber's kid taught me
what getting hit was all about
not so bad really
when you got used
to it and later
when it didn't bother me
much, I could wade through
almost anything and win
a pair of Rocky Marciano autographed
boxing gloves (my Dad at 92
doesn't recall where they went
or that they even were) and somehow
get myself into more fights
than any of my friends today
can imagine who never

even fought once.
Oh, what we will do to please
our daddies smiling shaking
hands for the camera following
commissioning second
lieutenants months before
leaving our daddies
to face other sons of daddies
in a place as unfamiliar
as that first exploding
roundhouse right to the ear.

LA CIUDAD DE LOS MUERTOS, CUBA
Maria Lisella

This is the Cadillac of cemeteries,
also called the Necropolis, he says,
Let us talk about the aristocracy.

Pedro hairless, round
half-man, half-boy
guides the uninitiated.

They are buried beneath
marble from Carrara, Italy,
France and quarries of Spain...

Pedro walks the cemetery daily
with groups of American travelers
visiting this soggy Cuban land.

But no matter, the important fact is
they may have been rich, but
now they are very, very dead.

Pablo knows he can impress them
with ghoulish details.
Even dying is complicated on this island,

It takes months for bodies to disintegrate
in Havana: two years for tendons to shrivel,
ossos are boxed, buried again

Two million rest here, outnumbered
the living at times in Havana, once
Chinese Coolie's plots, then opulent.

Like a circus barker in the center ring
One of the world's most luxurious cemeteries –
the others are in Buenos Aires, Paris, Genoa

We follow Pedro's steps like children.
under decayed Moorish gateways,
limestone images of faith and hope in Havana.

WE ARE IMMIGRANTS (this is not america)
James Tracy

italians
irish
english
portugese
french
german
we are immigrants
and this is not america

visas
braceros
green card
guest worker status
for who?
we are immigrants
and this is not america

propositions
immodest proposals
texas rangers
vigilantes
good old boys
we are immigrants
and this is not america

what we ran from
we become

conquerers
overseerers
persecutors
we are immigrants
and this is not america

please remember—
we need more john browns
than john kennedys

MACHINE SHOP
Jim Pignetti

slip past
factory door
dull light
greasy floor

play ball
hide and seek
run along
move your feet

get home
go to school
keep away
you're no fool

tick tock
don't stop
cinderblock
machine shop

thousand pounds
on the dock
hump the load
watch your back

mark it off
set the cut
feed the saw
pack it up

stainless steel
kick the shear

get it the fuck
outta here

I was the kid
I ran past
how'd this place
get my ass?

IT WAS CLEAR
Al Tacconelli

It was clear, they didn't stand a chance,
never did -- slowly closing in, they could
see weapons pointed towards death

provincial militia, like ravenous wolves,
surrounded them -- what they hoped and
prayed would never happen, happened

blindfolded eyes lost the world's light --
huddled against the village's crumbling
stone wall -- muffled weeping

to die in a rain of bullets repeatedly fired --
until flailing body parts ceased their quivering
-- bloody heap of gut splattered corpses

they had believed too much, were not worldly
wise enough to accept the new régime --
order of disorder, disguised as freedom.

POPOLO

People!

KEEP THE WHEAT AND LET THE CHAFF LIE
Mary Ann Mannino

There's an old pair of shoes
resting on the extension ladder
in my garage.
A pair of black Florsheim
wing tips, now scuffed, worn down in the heel
white paint splattered across the tops,
the lining of one torn and curled, the other missing.
They've been nesting on that ladder since 1980.
Twenty years I've cleaned that garage, spring and fall.
Forty times, I've returned them to their perch.
My papa's shoes.
Once proudly polished
preserved with metal shoe trees inside.

Papa never bought sneakers or casual clothes.
When his good clothes wore, he used them to
work around the house or yard. Once, he'd been
depression poor. Lost his house and sun-kissed fig tree.
Later, he spent money on beef roasts, schooling
for his children, books and bikes for my babies.
Throwing out old clothes, buying new ones for work
a frivolous waste.

These shoes he kept in my garage
along with frayed dress pants
a faded oxford shirt, a torn sweater.
He'd walk five blocks from his home to mine
impeccably dressed, not to embarrass me
before my neighbors. This gentle man
immigrant with broken tongue,
former farmer, friend of grape vines
olive trees, and sweet, black soil

displaced in a city.

He'd change clothes in my garage
sweep the leaves from my winding drive
nourish my azaleas with cow manure
weed my favorite flower beds
plant forsythia and hydrangeas he'd rooted
make my house and yard look loved,
richer than the houses of my neighbors
whose hired gardeners manicured their lawns.

No one's perfect.
My mother had stories.
My older brother too.
Mother used to say
"You don't know your father.
Once, he ripped his custom made
silk shirt in two because he lost a
button, and us with no money."
My older brother'd say about my parents
"When I was a boy, they'd go at it."
He'd shake his head.

But I know none of that.
I remember him legally blind at 80
gently lifting tomato seedlings he'd grown
as if they were eggshells or Waterford
placing them in rows in my garden
staking them with tree branches
he's stripped for the purpose
tying them with rags he'd uniformly cut
to save us money.

GARDENER
Edvige Giunta
for Cuciuzzo

He left
everything in order.
Neanche un filo d'erba, not a weed,
not a thread of grass.
Mother mourns the Sicilian garden.
Father hides behind words
that never betray.

Sixty-five years old when you died.
You were always sixty-five
and looking at your wrinkled face
I believed you were everybody's father,
including your wife, Carmelina,
who looked fifty at twenty,
withered by all those brothers
and clothes she washed in the pila
at the back of the house
with hard soap they don't sell in America.

In my aseptic condominium in Jersey City
washing machine and dryer
hide coyly behind white doors.
Carmelina's arms would be useless
in this country where clothes never
dance to the wind and clothespins
make only a rare, shy appearance
on a wooden rack in the bathtub
that quickly disappears into secret corners.

I am one of the old Italians dying
in the poem, trapped

between the half-life of chromium
sites beneath my house,
the flowers of New Jersey and the peaches of Gela
that turned black in my youth.
Yes, I am one of the old Italians,
and the fumes are taking my breath away.

In America you always die young,
whether you're fourteen, forty-four
or eighty-four, all deaths garnering
equal grief.

I spell birthday in my head
and a voice chants: the old Italians are dying.
My birthday a deathday.
One week after your funeral:
I blow out the candles and thirty-eight worms
court your flesh in the old cemetery,
where the old dead make room for the new
in tight alcoves.

You tricked me, he says.
But who is the trickster, who, the magician?
And what if you don't know
the words that will undo your spells?
What if in the solitude of the Garden State
all you can smell is the aroma of death
and the only guests at your party
are the old Italians dancing
a tarantella inside your heart?

IN MY NEIGHBORHOOD
Giovanna Capone

the smell of roasting peppers
was often floating in the air
as Mr. Bonavitacola sizzled them
over an outdoor flame,
the sweet aroma drifting to every nose.

You would often hear the loud buzz
of an electric saw
as the Nardone's next door
knocked down a wall

With hammer and nails
they'd sheet rock a second bedroom
extending their front porch
to accommodate their bursting family.

In my neighborhood
people re-built their homes from scratch
Old toilets sat
on sidewalks
Tomato plants sprang up
on the slivers of land
between sidewalk and street
The neighbors were at it again.
We thought of them as ginzos, right off the boat
They came from Italy
as we did,
only more recently.

They moved in next door
and next door
and next door

till one by one, all down the block the dagos flocked
and our neighborhood became
a Little Italy, of sorts
They moved in next door, leaving their families
an ocean behind

They'd fix up dumpy houses
working their asses off
the whole family sawing hammering building
till they made it halfway good
Home sweet home

They sent their kids to American schools
Gli bambini non hanno parlato italiano.
Only at home, would they eat Italian food
and speak Italian words.
Le parole italiane vivevano solo nella casa.

The Italians in our neighborhood
kept a distance from the Americans
and their strange ways
their broken families, disrespectful kids,
and politicians full of lies
They could never quite trust
questo mondo degli americani
where nothing is superior to
the almighty dollar bill

But in America they could
find a job,
buy a broken down house
and make it home.
They could squeak out a way to live

Yet decades later, if you ever asked them,

they'd still say
"Mi famiglia sono di Napoli, Sicilia, Calabria,
Avellino."
They'd still say
"Sono Italiano."

---

* The children did not speak Italian.
 * Italian words lived only in the home.
   * this world of the Americans

SPAGHETTI CON MELANZANE
Michael Cirelli
for Sara

Nothing better than homemade spaghetti—
Nothing better than that spaghetti with a good
sauce, (that doesn't have to be cooked by your Nonna),
but has to be cooked long long long, so long the skin
on the fruit dissolves, so long the oil in the pot
gets red-tinted – or nothing better than that spaghetti
in an Aglio e Olio, or in a Cacio e Pepe – or that Spaghetti
con Melanzane, and the melanzane no longer resembles
melanzane after it marries with onion-garlic-plum-
tomatoes, and is consecrated by flame, and the melanzane
now has a certain "give" on the teeth, a certain softness
or easing up, and there's nothing better than that melanzane
matched with this homemade spaghetti, matched with you—
sitting across from me, with a long strand of pasta dangling
from your soft puckered lips.

THE POW
James Vescovi

My grandfather, Tony, was drafted into the Italian army at seventeen. When the officers noted his strength and his propensity to follow orders, they made him a Bersagliere, the Italian equivalent of a U.S. Marine. The term comes from a verb meaning "to harass, or badger."

Tony saw a good deal of action in the trenches during World War I, though he bitterly pointed out that when an Italian soldier was ordered to charge enemy lines, most commanding officers stayed behind. They were recruited from the coddled upper class, said my grandfather, a peasant from Emilia-Romagna. Judging from his experience, my guess is that he was captured at the Battle of Caporetto. It was a military disaster for Italy. More than 275,000 soldiers were captured, while another 300,000 troops deserted.

He and his comrades were marched eastward for three weeks to a POW camp in Hungary. Under the eye of an especially cruel Italian sergeant who brokered a deal with the enemy, the prisoners worked 12-hour days on farms and ate a miserable gruel. Tony escaped three times and was recaptured twice. He returned the last time because he was starving and could find no quarter with the Hungarian peasants.

He was not released until 1920, two years after the signing of the Armistice. It took him and other enlisted men several months to find their own way to Trieste, where the Italian government had set up a facility to repatriate soldiers. Tony was then shipped south to Naples to another staging point. A few months passed before he reached home in the Apennine Mountains west of Parma.

For Tony, the only good thing that came from military service was a check he received in 1922 for three years of back pay. It funded his emigration to New York. His passport cost the equivalent of $10 and described his eyes as "castagna" (chestnut).

Until he died at ninety-four, he received a veteran's check from the Italian government twice a year. He personally went to the Italian Consulate at Park Avenue and 68th Street to pick it up. The checks didn't amount to much—about $160 each—but he wanted what was coming to him.

Toward the end of his life, Tony developed a serious vision problem. One day as my father and I were going through his parents' mail, he held up Tony's pension check and said, "Thanks for picking this up at the Consulate."

"I didn't pick it up," I said.

"Did it come in the mail?"

I shook my head.

My father looked over at his father, who was lying on the couch for his post-lunch siesta. "Pa, did someone bring you your pension check?"

Tony shook his head.

"How did it get here?"

Tony shrugged.

That meant only one thing: The old man took two subways, found his way to the Consulate, claimed his check, and returned home, without being able to see ten feet in front of him.

On a business trip my father once visited a Bersagliere museum in Rome. When he told the docent he was the son of a Bersagliere, he was given a VIP tour. At the end, my father, knowing that Tony had thrown away his military ribbons long ago, asked whether it might be possible to get a new set (though he told the docent the originals were "lost").

"Of course! Of course!" replied the docent, himself a Bersagliere. "All I need is his full name and serial number. I will take care of it personally!"

When my father reported the news to his father, Tony said, "No. No ribbons, nothing!"

LA MIA CUGINA
Gabriella Belfiglio

I meet Gina Maria at the Capitol Hilton,

she's sitting with two of her best friends—
the last time I saw these women we were all wearing
the same dress. Honeydew green, strapless, big skirt.
All night it was hard to breathe in that thing.

The four of us go to an Italian restaurant, Giovanni's,
only a few streets away. Still, they call a cab, file in.
No one but me is wearing shoes they can walk in.

At dinner Gina and I sit next to each other—
laughter spreading like olive oil between us.
She tells me the story of her husband's home-
made cherry pie, of candles lit throughout the bed-
room, of passion fruit massage oil, and the platinum
and diamond necklace—three times.

Don't you think I married the right man—
I mean who the hell else would bake for them?

In high school she used to sit behind me in Italian class,
when our teacher was turned away she would
poke me and whisper my name, as he turned
back it is I who would get yelled at—not being
able to hold the smile from my mouth.

Giovanni himself is our waiter
everything the small man does is big
he bounces over to us   so many beautiful
girls at one table—how can thisa be? maybe you
need me to join you, no?
When he brings fresh parmesan to top our pasta

it comes in wild torrents
more cheese ends up on our laps than on the plates
—a little more a little more—he says with each thrust.

Giovanni can't keep his eyes off
Gina's necklace slipping into her cleavage—
three large diamonds lighting up her cardinal chest.

Gina and I finish the dinners of the other two—
we have been trained to eat like others are taught
to cover their mouths when they cough.

The conversation moves to politics.
When I realize I am the only one
who does not have the thought that
our Pakistani taxi driver might be a terrorist
I know it is time for me to leave.

Sometimes blood is only as thick as tomato sauce.

IL RANCORE
Bliss Esposito

Italians are the only people I know who can love so deeply they'll never speak to someone again. My dad loved his dog Trooper so much he killed the mutt himself before Animal Control could take it away for biting the lip off the little girl next door. I love my family so much I've become a writer in order to write their spirits into tangibility. That way I'll still have them when they're gone, and, consequently, I have no time for them while they're still here.

Obsession is just one of the stereotypes Italian Americans are forced to deal with. Crime, violence and infidelity are high on the list, too. Even as a young, educated woman generations away from any actual danger or repression, people constantly ask about my "connections." It's infuriating at times—and it makes me want to stab them in the ear with an ice pick—nonetheless, our stereotypes come from a genuine sample. We are a people of grudge, emotion, and mania. It's ingrained in us to love and protect and be there forever, but when our honorable intentions are thwarted, we just can't help ourselves. Our blood is set to boil, and we do everything we can to avoid losing the ones we love, even if it means choking them to death ourselves.

Take, for example, my uncle Lenny. Uncle Lenny wants to smash his right knee with a hammer. He has already cursed all the saints in heaven, and vowed that when he goes to "that big casino in the sky," he's going to "punch God right in the head." He repeats with emphasis, "in the head." He recently found out that he is going to need a second reconstructive surgery on his knee, and it is not going over well. The walls of his home have been vibrating with impressive forms of obscenity and blasphemy, the likes of which the quiet Sun City community in the ritzy part of Las Vegas has never heard. His walker was thrown against the cherry-wood cabinet of guns and gun books and awards for shooting guns in a fit of rage, making the little bronze-colored dogs next door yap relentlessly (which made Lenny even madder because he hates "those friggin' rats"). The brace given to him after the first surgery was ceremoniously pulled off, bitten and ripped at, but thanks to the medical-grade rubber he'll be able to use it again. The future is bleak for Lenny right now. He wonders if he'll still be able to take his family on vacation this summer. He thinks he will ask his doctor about medication for depression. He doesn't know why he never found a broad to marry that didn't drive him nuts. His busted knee is a tragedy.

But his busted knee might be just what we need to save the family.

It's a long story of short tempers.

Lenny hasn't spoken to his twin brother Franky in twelve years, and my father, mother, sister and I have all been in the middle. We took it for granted that our little knot was stable so many years ago, when Grandma would place name cards on our plates at Sunday dinner, even though we always sat in the same spots. We would eat marinara and meatballs, and Lenny would splatter sauce on his cleanly pressed shirt no matter what precautions he may have taken: a napkin, a handkerchief, a lead shield, it didn't matter. Franky might playfully hold a butcher knife to Lenny's neck, blade away from skin. Grandma would scream. Grandpa would hit Dad in the head with a slipper for saying something off-color at the dinner table. We would laugh. Brooklyn accents would flair around the room, and I'd practice saying "tree" instead of "three" so I could lay claim to my heritage. We were eight, then six after my grandparents passed away, but always our own little island in a growing city with fewer and fewer of our *fratelli* and *sorelle* who understood just what the word *famiglia* meant. And then we split, too.

On one side of the feud is Lenny, his heart too big for his too big body. He started his career of taking care of the family early, always looking out for his brothers. Once, as a kid, my dad "accidentally" ripped off some fur coats from the Profaci mob. (Okay, so maybe there are a few genuine mafia moments.) Lenny smacked Dad upside the head and took the coats back himself, apologizing for his idiot kid brother. The guys understood and nobody lost any knuckles over it. Lenny keeps it together, stays calm when his brothers can't. His fuse is the longest, but when he blows it's worse than any display at the Nevada Test Sight. He says "Thank you" when my sister and I say "I love you" and reaches for his wallet when he senses any tension in the family. You lost your job? Here go take the kids out to dinner. You need surgery? Here go get your car detailed. You had a miscarriage? Don't worry,

Sweetheart. Uncle Lenny's gonna buy you a brand new couch.

Then there's shiftily skinny Franky, the same face, but with a gap between his front teeth and a whole different set of values. Franky couldn't keep up with Lenny monetarily, though he has been known to lay a C-note or even a G on one of us nieces in times of distress. In the sixties, he did six years in the joint where he stuffed mattresses with Jimmy Hoffa. (Okay, maybe there are more than a few actual mob moments.) In prison he became a Jehovah's Witness. He has since spent the rest of his life passing out pamphlets, knocking on doors and otherwise preparing for the end of the world. He took all of his money out of the bank and stopped paying taxes. He doesn't technically "own" anything. Try to take something that's his, though, and watch the hell out. He attempted to convince his brothers to give up their ties to Catholicism and become one of the 144,000 that would be saved at the Second Coming. No one ever believed him, really, but my parents still have sacks of wheat and 20-gallon bottles of water in the garage for the day we need to pack it up and move into the hills. Just in case. Franky doesn't know how the world will end (though he thinks the Jews will have something to do with it), but it's going to happen. He'll be ready. Still, he's getting anxious. Time is slipping by, and he might not get to hear the trumpets. Lately, he's been saying that if the world doesn't end soon, he's just going to go ahead and get the kitchen retiled.

There have been tremors of tension between the identical twins since they fought to be first out of the womb (Franky won, and it still pisses Lenny off), but we can trace their falling out back to a single incident. Lenny wanted to buy some property, and he said he'd buy the house Franky rented if the landlord ever wanted to sell. Franky with his piety and paranoia always expected his big brother Lenny to be there to lean on—to co-sign when Franky couldn't establish credit, to pick up the tab, to bail him out if he got into a jam—so this was a perfect plan. Years went by. Lenny bought other houses to rent. When Franky's house finally did go up for sale, Lenny didn't have the liquid, and Franky had to scramble to pull some money together. Franky was outraged. Forget the Jews, he'd been screwed by his own brother. That was twelve years ago and they haven't talked since.

Of course, we never thought it would last. How many fights had they been in before? Over money, over broads, over space, over time. They always made up, or at least got distracted enough to forget they were fighting. Why would this one be any different? They, along with my dad, formed an indisputable image of what it means to be a man for me—all muscles and brawn with an ironic penchant for romance and tenderness—undoubtedly screwing up my own relationships and expectations. I remember my dad setting up folding chairs in front of our turtle's tank so they could drop an unsuspecting goldfish in and watch the turtle tear it to shreds. Sometimes I'd hide in my room with my ears plugged against the sounds of their cheering, other times I'd choose a knee to sit on and cheer along myself. I remember them getting ready to go shooting in the desert like they were packing in for Nam. And the stories that came out of their adventures: the time Franky pinged a few BBs off the water tower Lenny was climbing ("...you ain't never seen that fat ass move so quick in his life!"), the time they executed my sister's bunny because he ate my dad's pot plant ("...the little prick had it coming"), the time they had to walk in ten miles from the desert because Lenny beat his car to death with a baseball bat ("...").

They were each other's link to the past. Once a whole country, then just cities, a neighborhood, a street, my home. For my family, the Italian-American culture was siphoning down to just me and my sister: a couple of half-breeds who mediated arguments and pronounced "th" correctly. When the word was out that Franky and Lenny were no longer speaking, the wonderfully rich and beautiful tradition of our family, our ancestors, a clan that had already survived two migrations—one to the original Ellis Island and one to "Ellis Island" advertising $1.99 steak and eggs, lounge acts and dollar beers—was in danger. It was a new time for us. We had to relearn how to have vacations and dinners. The uncles, who had always traveled together—a twosome, a couple, a duet—now had to be queued. Holiday meals were spent in six hour spreads: Uncle Lenny arriving two hours early and Uncle Franky two hours late (after the Watchtower meetings, of course). If my grandparents were still alive they wouldn't have stood for it. If they were married their wives wouldn't have stood for it. Give a couple of hot-headed men free reign over their lives and this is what happens.

I couldn't believe it. I'd always felt so superior to my friends in the fact that I liked my family, and ours was one that worked. Maybe the plates of pasta and vats of tomato sauce were a little cliché; still, we never thought to do anything different. But now I was just angry. This stupid rift between my uncles was causing the breakdown of the raucous stability I'd always known. I was only fifteen when it started and couldn't really understand the gravity of the situation, both for them and for us. Now at a point so much later, when I can look at them with the objectivity that comes with more experience, I realize the other side of the passion we feel about things. Whether it's family or food or money or sex, we live so deeply it's almost counterproductive to life. We shouldn't make decisions that will last forever while we are crazed. But we do. That level of intensity cannot be maintained forever. Maybe that's how the rest of the world does it. If you're only living at a four you can't fall too far. But keep it at ten too long, and you're in for a hell of a drop.

A few years ago, Uncle Lenny took us to Hawaii. He'd wanted to take us on a family trip for years, but scheduling was rough: my parents still worked, I was finishing my Masters degree, and my sister and her husband were on a strict regiment of hormones and shots for infertility. But Lenny got us all pinned down, finally, and booked us on a trip of a lifetime. He's a world traveler, himself, and wherever he goes he buys me, my mom and my sister identical pieces of jewelry. We have pewter from Greece, porcelain from Russia, and jade from Japan.

His traveling began late in life. A deep depression had set in on him fueled by loneliness and television watching after he retired. His twin brother was no longer in his life, someone he'd spent over six decades taking care of. He'd never married or had kids; I suspect he was a little jealous of my dad for settling down. Lenny suddenly found himself with nothing to do, except to lie on his couch all day, and in crept the reality of his waning days. So he began a new life of adventure.

This adventure he wanted share with all of us. He booked everything high end, from the hotel, to the rooms, to the view, to the tours, to the limo service at the airport....

To each of the different planes.

"You and your boyfriend," he said to me as he spread the tickets across the table, two airlines, two sets, "will be flying with your mommy and your daddy. And your sister and her husband will be going with me."

"We're on separate planes?" my sister asked. She and I looked at each other. We should have seen this coming.

"Well, we've got to be sure that if one of the planes goes down, someone will get the inheritance." He shuffled the tickets and handed us an itinerary. "I don't want anything going to that ungrateful brother of mine."

It's not like we're the Rockefellers, I said.

God couldn't resist taking us all out at once, Lenny confirmed.

It was funny that Lenny actually thought it a viable concern that God would specifically make a plane with the whole family on it go down and that Franky would get all his money. That Lenny would kill half of us or himself just to prove a point to his brother. To go to his grave screaming *vaffanculo*, happily giving everything he owned to anyone but his brother.

I'm terrified of flying, so this little "precaution" didn't help. On the flight, my mom had to take a Valium because she's claustrophobic, and my dad took an Ambien and a couple of Lortabs because he was bored. I sat next to my boyfriend, who I wasn't speaking to because he refused to stop reading *The Times* and talk to me. I felt absolutely sure that we would end up in a steaming mass of rubble halfway between the islands and the coast. We would die, and they would live or vice versa. I wondered what would be worse, a few minutes of terror replaced by a quick and sudden darkness, or a lifetime of wishing it was the other way around. What had he done by splitting us up? How could inheritance possibly matter when air masks are dropping like nooses, and you're trying to remember what the fuck to do with seat cushion? Uncle Lenny was insane, crazy, completely *pazzo*. If one of us was going to have to go down, I would rather we all just go down together.

We're not sociopaths, as the media would like people to believe. We're completely the opposite. In an age of remorseless criminals, our crimes and our anger come from the exact same place as our devotion and honor. It may become hard to distinguish the stereotype from real life when you have family members that actually say fuggetaboutit even though they haven't watched a mob flick made after 1974. The mythic idea of the Italian American was based on something real. It's reductive and insulting, but looking at my own family as a realistic example of Italian Americans, I can't deny that there is an eerie resonance to the stereotype. We break rules and flip out unnecessarily. Perhaps we could take our feelings down a notch or two. We could ignore our hurt and keep relationships breathing. We could sit quietly. We could refuse the urge to punch that guy in the face. We could keep our hands to ourselves and not grab the ones we adore. We could stand still for a change. We could get less excited about eating. We could stifle our cries and our laughter. We could forget where we came from.

Fuggetaboutit.

Uncle Lenny had his second knee surgery recently. In the hospital room he told the nurse that when he healed, he was going to beat the shit out of the hospital cook. He was dead serious. At home, he is a terrible patient. Dad is going nuts trying to keep him on his back or in his brace. Lenny already destroyed the first surgery because he was up walking around too soon. There is something terrifying and reminiscent to Lenny about lying on the couch for so long. It makes him regret things and think too hard. He refuses to drink water and even though the doctors told him that the area connecting the ligament to the bone is as thin as tissue paper, Uncle Lenny still insists on getting to the refrigerator on his own.

My poor dad wants to strangle him. He won't leave his bedside, but Lenny is proving to be impossible. He complains. He's upset. He wants to kill people and saints alike. He's convinced that he is cursed. The doctors said if he doesn't settle down, he may end up in a wheelchair for the rest of his life. He's 75 now. It could be twenty years. It could be tomorrow.

It's in these times when mortality faces us that the hurt is the worst.

The other day Dad talked to Franky. He told Franky what the doctors said. Franky knows how Lenny can get and even though they don't speak he said to wish him well. Dad told Franky to be the bigger man and call his brother. He also told Lenny to be the bigger man and give Franky a chance. It's possible. They are both softening. They know the age and wear they feel in their own bodies is happening to their brother. And even if they can't admit it of themselves, they know that their twin can only have a few good years left. This surgery has put a vein of mortality through all of us. It was cold, dark and hidden before. Now it pulses and demands attention, making us analyze things that we didn't want to have to think about yet. There isn't time for petty bullshit. Our chance to be a family again is getting smaller and smaller each day. When once we thought that they couldn't keep this up forever, we now realize that only one kind of forever stretches before us, and whether it's Jehovah, or Jesus, or just plain nothing, once one of them beats the other to the finish line, their opportunity to mature and make new memories to add to the old ones will be gone. Forever.

In a few months, Uncle Lenny is taking us to Alaska. We're flying up to Seattle where we will board a cruise liner. As we board our separate planes, I'll be thankful that at least he trusts God enough to put us on the same ship. I'll be with my parents because I'm the baby of the family, and my sister, her husband and my niece will be flying with him. Hopefully by then Lenny's knee will be healed, because the Espositos don't really like airports all that much, and if someone tries to put him in an airport wheelchair or dust his cane for explosives, there's going to be trouble. Maybe Uncle Lenny is right: we have an obligation to save half the family if possible, but as far as inheritance goes, Lenny's money would be packed in a box and shipped to the moon before, legally, Uncle Franky could claim it. I don't know that they will ever make up. I do know, however, that the passion we feel is a beautiful gift, and even though sometimes it erupts in smudges and stains, it's worth it. We're tough. I'm sure both planes will be safe. Still, if one of them is destined to go down, and I suddenly find myself sitting on a mountain of my uncle's gold, I know I'd trade it for the chance that all of us, completed, could sit together one more time.

And if Uncle Lenny does make it to heaven, God better run.

CHICKPEAS
Maria Fama

This is how we pass down our history
hold up a handful of chickpeas
say "cíceri" in Sicilian tongue

This is how we pass down our history
through the ages
whether we could read or write or not
in countryside   mountainside   seaside

This is how we pass down our history
my father holds up a handful of roasted chickpeas
makes us repeat the word after him
"cíceri" "cíceri" "cíceri"
we are children anxious to leave the table
play   laugh   shout   in English
in Philadelphia   USA
where our family set down roots
fragile and tough as chickpea plants

we were Mediterranean for millennia
          American for two decades

This is how we pass down our history
my father holds up a handful of roasted chickpeas
this night they are snacks with wine
my grandfather tells us we should always have
a handful of chickpeas in our pocket as he does
in case we get hungry
in case we are served food we cannot eat
the chickpeas will sustain us
"cíceri" "cíceri" "cíceri"
say "cíceri" "cíceri" "cíceri"

My father holds up a handful of chickpeas
this humble exalted Mediterranean food
in a Philadelphia kitchen
we must learn to say
"cíceri" "cíceri" "cíceri"

This is how we pass down our history
over the centuries across oceans
countryside mountainside seaside

My father tells us the history of the proud and oppressed
in 1282 the Sicilians rose up
against the arrogant haughty French
who taxed and insulted the Sicilian people
took liberties with Sicilian women
lounged in Sicilian homes

Sicilians were patient waiting for their chance
to overthrow the French
the chance came on Easter Monday in Palermo
in front of the Church of the Holy Spirit
the armed French soldiers stood guard
over the Palermitans thronging the piazza
as they headed to the Church's Vespers service
the French soldier Drouette, filled with Sicilian wine,
stopped a beautiful young woman
walking to church with her husband
Drouette grabbed her as if to search for weapons
fondled her breasts
her husband shouted "Death to the French!"
the crowd surged the fighting began
Drouette fell stabbed in the heart

Messengers carried the signal throughout the island
the time had come "Death to the French!"

Sicilians rose up
with knives, rocks, sticks, stones, canes, swords
west to east   east to west
north to south   south to north
"Death to the French!"
thousands of French hunted down and killed
as the signal traveled the island's
countryside   mountainside   seaside

My father tells us some French tried to escape
dressed in peasant clothes
they hid in countryside   mountainside   seaside
they were caught and killed my father says
my grandfather holds up a handful of chickpeas
says "cíceri" "cíceri" "cíceri"
my father says the French could not pronounce the word correctly
"cíceri" "cíceri" "cíceri"
humble   exalted   powerful   chickpeas

"cíceri" "cíceri" "cíceri"

If you were Sicilian you said "cíceri"
if you were Sicilian
Go in Peace   The Madonna Bless You
in your countryside   mountainside   seaside   home
you lived on to bless
the exalted   humble   powerful
"cíceri" "cíceri" "cíceri"

This is how we pass down our history
my father and grandfather holding chickpeas in their palms
telling us how Sicilians chopped up French dead
shipped them back to France pickled in barrels

our skin goosebumps as we listen
our eyes widen with horror and wonder

think how it would be if Sicilians held up chickpeas
they would kill you if you did not say it right
"cíceri" "cíceri" "cíceri"
you feel sorry for those French
sent to a faraway land where they were hated
where they could not pronounce
"cíceri" "cíceri" "cíceri"

you feel relief as you say
"cíceri" "cíceri" "cíceri"
you would live and be sustained by
humble exalted powerful chickpeas

you are proud
as you take a handful of roasted chickpeas
eat them slowly
your father and grandfather smile
when you say "cíceri" "cíceri" "cíceri"
because even though you live in Philadelphia USA
your family was saved nearly eight hundred years ago
in countryside mountainside seaside
when they said "cíceri" "cíceri" "cíceri"
therefore, this is how we must pass down our history
hold up a handful of chickpeas
say "cíceri" in Sicilian tongue.

BREAD STORY: The Blessings of Private Enterprise
Michael Parenti

Years ago, my father drove a delivery truck for the Italian bakery owned by his uncle Torino. When Zi Torino returned to Italy in 1956, my father took over the entire business. The bread he made was the same bread that had been made in Gravina, Italy, for generations. After a whole day standing, it was fresh as ever, the crust having grown hard and crisp while the inside remained soft, solid, and moist. People used to say that our bread was a meal in itself.

The secret of the bread had been brought by my Zi Torino all the way from the Mediterranean to Manhattan, down into the tenement basement where he had installed wooden vats and tables. The bakers were two dark wiry men, paesani di Gravina, who rhythmically and endlessly pounded their powdery white hands into the dough, molding the bread with strength and finesse. Zi Torino and then my father after him, used time and care in preparing their bread, letting the dough sit and rise naturally, turning it over twice a night, using no chemicals and only the best quality unbleached flour. The bread was baked slowly and perfectly in an old brick oven built into the basement wall by Zi Torino in 1907, an oven that had secrets of its own.

Often during my college days, I would assist my father in loading up the bread truck at 5:00 a.m. on Saturday mornings. We delivered in the Bronx to Italian families whose appreciation for good bread was one of the satisfactions of our labor. My father's business remained small but steady. Customers, acquired slowly by word of mouth, remained with us forever. He would engage them in friendly conversations as he went along his route, taking nine hours to do seven hours of work. He could tell me more than I wanted to know about their family histories.

In time, some groceries, restaurants, and supermarkets started placing orders with us, causing us to expand our production. My father seemed pleased by the growth in his business. But after some months, one of his new clients, the Jerome Avenue Supermarket did the unexpected. The supermarket's manager informed my father that one of the big companies, Wonder Bread, was going into the "specialty line" and was offering to take over the Italian bread account. As an inducement to the supermarket, Wonder Bread was promising a free introductory offer of two hundred loaves. With that peculiar kind of generosity often found in merchants and bosses, the supermarket manager offered to reject the bid and keep our account if only we would match Wonder Bread's offer at least in part, say a hundred loaves.

"Their bread is paper compared to mine," my father protested. Indeed, our joke was: the reason they call it Wonder Bread is because after tasting it, you wonder if it's bread. But his artisan's pride proved no match for the merchant's manipulations, and he agreed to deliver a hundred free loaves, twenty-five a day, in order to keep the supermarket account, all the while cursing the manager under his breath. In the business world, this arrangement is referred to as a "deal" or an "agreement." To us it seemed more like extortion.

In response to "deals" of this sort, my father developed certain tricks of his own. By artfully flashing his hands across the tops of the delivery boxes he would short count loaves right under the noses of the store managers, in the case of the Jerome Avenue Supermarket, even loaves that they finally started paying for again. "Five and five across, that's twenty-five, Pete," he would point out, when in fact it was only twenty-three. We would load 550 loaves for the morning run and he would sell 575. Not since the Sermon on the Mount had the loaves so increased.

"Pop," I said to him after one of his more daring performances, "You're becoming a thief."

"Kid," he said, "It's no sin to steal from them that steal from you."[Individual competition in the pursuit of private gain brings out the best of our creative energies and thereby maximizes our productive contributions and advances the well being of the entire society. Economics 101]

I left for a few years to go to graduate school, only to return home in 1959 without a penny in my pocket. I asked my father to support me for a semester so that I could finish writing my dissertation. In return, I offered to work a few days a week on the bread truck. My father agreed to this but he wondered how he would explain to friends and neighbors that his son was twenty-six years old and still without full-time employment.

"Kid, how long can you keep going to school and what for?" he asked. "All those books," he would warn me, "are bad for your eyes and bad for your mind."

"Well," I said, "I'm getting a Ph.D." To this he made no response. So I put in a few days a week of hard labor on the truck. Nor did he complain. In fact, he needed the help and liked having me around (as he told my stepmother who told me).

When the bakers asked him how come, at the age of twenty-six, I was working only part-time, he said: "He's getting a Ph.D." From then on they called me "professor," a term that was applied with playful sarcasm. It was their way of indicating that they were not as impressed with my intellectual efforts as some people might be.

On the day my dissertation was accepted and I knew I was to receive my Ph.D., I proudly informed my father. He nodded and said, "That's good." Then he asked me if I wanted to become a full-time partner in the bread business working with him on the truck every day. With all the education out of the way, now maybe I would be ready to do some real work.

I almost said yes.

One day the health inspectors came by and insisted we could not leave the bread naked in stores in open display boxes, exposed to passers-by who might wish to touch or fondle the loaves with their germ-ridden fingers. No telling what kind of infected predators might chance into a supermarket to fondle bread. So my father and I were required to seal each loaf in a plastic bag, thus increasing our production costs, adding hours to our labor, and causing us to handle the bread twice as much with our germ-carrying fingers. But now it looked and tasted like modern bread because the bags kept the moisture in, and the loaves would get gummy in their own humidity inside their antiseptic plastic skins instead of forming a crisp, tasty crust in the open air.

Then some of the bigger companies began in earnest to challenge our restaurant and store trade, underselling us with an inferior quality "Italian bread." At about this time the price of flour went up. Then the son of the landlord from whom Zi Torino had first rented the bakery premises over a half century before raised our rent substantially.

"When it rains it pours," my father said. So he tried to reduce costs by giving the dough more air and water and spending less time on the preparation. The bakers shook their heads and went on making the imitation product for the plastic bags.

"Pop," I complained, "the bread doesn't taste as good as it used to. It's more like what the Americans make."

"What's the difference? They still eat it, don't they?" he said with a tight face.

But no matter what he did, things became more difficult. Some of our old family customers complained about the change in the quality of the bread and began to drop their accounts. And a couple of the big stores decided it was more profitable to carry the commercial brands.

Not long after, my father disbanded the bakery and went to work driving a cab for one of the big taxi fleets in New York City. In all the years that followed, he never mentioned the bread business again.

GENERATIONS
Kim Addonizio

Somewhere a shop of hanging meats,
shop of stink and blood, block and cleaver;

somewhere an immigrant, grandfather, stranger
with my last name. That man

untying his apron in 1910, scrubbing off
the pale fat, going home past brownstones

and churches, past vendors, streetcars, arias,
past the clatter of supper dishes, going home

to his new son, my father—
What is he to me, butcher with sausage fingers,

old Italian leaning over a child somewhere
in New York City, somewhere alive, what is he

that I go back to look for him, years after his death
and my father's death, knowing only

a name, a few scraps my father fed me?
My father who shortened that name, who hacked off

three lovely syllables, who raised American children.
What is the past to me

that I have to go back, pronouncing that word
in the silence of a cemetery, what is this stone

coming apart in my hands like bread, name
I eat and expel? Somewhere the smell of figs

and brine, strung garlic, rosemary and olives;
somewhere that place. Somewhere a boat

rocking, crossing over, entering the harbor. I wait
on the dock, one face in a crowd of faces.

Families disembark and stream toward the city,
and though I walk among them for hours,

hungry, haunting the streets,
I can't tell which of them is mine.

Somewhere a steak is wrapped in thick paper,
somewhere my grandmother is laid in the earth,

and my young father shines shoes on a corner,
turning his back to the old world, forgetting.

I walk the night city, looking up at lit windows,
and there is no table set for me, nowhere

I can go to be filled. This is the city
of grandparents, immigrants, arrivals,

where I've come too late with my name,
an empty plate. This is the place.

PIEVE, LIGURE
Linda Simone

My sister can't speak
the name of this ancient Italian town.
 Pave Liguro
 or *Pavia Liguria*, she says. And we laugh.

Hard to say, harder still to find,
nestled down two-way cobble streets
the width of driveways
trestled between Bogliasco and Recco.

At Pontetto station,
we learn patience
wait – sometimes one half-hour –
for trains to whistle their *arrivederci*
and the red-striped arm to salute
so we can cross tracks.

Just two days ...and this town,
however you say it,
is in our blood.

RACHELE'S POCKETBOOK FRITTATA
Annie Rachele Lanzilotto

My mother carries a frittata wherever she goes. It's because of paranoia and a Depression era "wolf at the door" mentality. To invite her out to eat is inviting a nervous breakdown. To her credit, she'll take five milligrams of Xanax and try. My downtown haunts she raises her eyebrows at, saying, "filthy." The only place she will eat fish is the cafeteria at Sloan-Kettering; they cured me of cancer twice there, her once. That's where last Columbus Day when we got our back-to-back colonoscopies, she announced to the handsome doctor, "Don't you make any new discoveries today, Columbus discovered enough!"

Since Columbus Day has become torturous for me as an Italian American who has listened to Native Americans' lament, anger, and dismissal of white ethnics who celebrate, I have felt blindsided by my own upbringing and have had to do some ethnic cleansing on myself. Ethnic cleansing's okay, as long as you're doing it on yourself.

I got so much satisfaction fasting and purging and opening my anus up for the camera on Columbus Day that I decided to make it my personal annual ritual. In between our routine surveillance check-ups, my mother wipes her hands with the antibacterial formula hanging in dispensers on the Sloan-Kettering walls, looks down at the floors with a smile, pecan-crusted trout, "Great," she says licking the plastic fork and throw-away plate.

Other than that and an occasional bagel (the only thing in the city she justifies ordering), she will not spend money out on food, "I can't see it," she says, especially anything she can make herself at home. Pasta is out. Nonetheless, I try to get her out of the kitchen and into the city.

We've had plenty of what I call "Kitchen Trauma Drama." The kitchen is the site of creation and destruction in our family. The kitchen is where we summon life and take up swords with death. The kitchen, where my crib was kept, where my mother was posted night and day over the hot stove, sopre il forno caldo, where our ancestors enter in the dark hours when I can't sleep and sit peering into the white light of the great open 'frigerator, the kitchen where my mother dipped hundreds of cigarettes into the gas blue flames with her teeth, the kitchen where my father beat her, the kitchen where the wall of her aorta split, where the constant water of the faucet runs calling to me our Acquaviva delle Fonte fountains. Yes, where the running water makes me feel atavistically at home. The kitchen I try to get my mother out of, as often as I can. And so, she will leave, but not without a frittata.

I ask her of her pocketbook frittata recipe: "First you get the phone call, 'Ma, how bout meetin' us downtown?' And before you look up the bus schedule, you look in the fridge to see what's there. I open up the fridge, I see there's some asparagus, onion, parsley, cheese: swiss and pecorino romano and sharp cheddar. How many eggs? I get out the big frying pan. On goes the gas. I start the onion. I beat up as many eggs as I have. 4 to 8. The onions caramelize. I drop in the asparagus. I throw in the parsley, cheese, if there's a little mozzarell I throw it in. Depending on the bus schedule I eliminate potatoes, or I use frozen home fries if there's any hanging out in the freezer. If you cut potatoes, thin! If a few mushrooms, throw them in. When brown, add eggs and cheese. A little drop of cold water to the eggs. Go all around the edge of the pan with a spatula to loosen it. Tip the frying pan side to side. Let the extra liquid lead onto the pan. When fairly firm, get a plate a little larger than the pan, take the pan off the stove, flip the pan on the plate (but today they have hundred dollar pans that won't burn in the oven) slide frittata back into the pan from the plate. Make sure it's firm enough otherwise you'll have it dripping down your legs. Let it cool while you get dressed for downtown. Wrap it in tin foil and a dish towel. Of course, you gotta have the right pocketbook. Run for the bus. All the way downtown I get a nice smell like I'm in a restaurant on the bus. As the bus pulls into 23rd Street I see a smiling face from a car. Somebody's out there waiting for the frittata. P.S. if you have broccoli florets, leftover spinach, Italian frying peppers, zucchini..."

ETHIOPIA
Gil Fagiani

Nonna fed me pastina with escarole
bought me ices and slices of focaccia
calmed my cough with spoonfuls of honey.

When she eyed my bandaged head
after Butchie Malizzio hit me with a rock
she shamed my father into making Butchie lay off.

Years later I found out she sent Mussolini
her wedding ring to finance the war machine
that bombed and gassed the Ethiopians into submission.

Povera nonna,
like Christopher Columbus
she's lost her saintly luster.

VEAL SCALOPPINI
Kim Nicolini

"You want milk, baby? You get milk." Pat snaps his fingers and tells the waiter to bring me some milk.

The waiter brings over a glass of milk in a cocktail glass with a skinny red straw stuck inside. He puts the milk in front of me and tells me it will give me beautiful skin. "I can see the milk in your skin," the waiter tells me. "So beautiful, soft and white." He leans right into my face and winks.

Sure, my skin is soft. I'm sixteen years old. Sixteen-year-old girls usually have soft skin.

It's 1978, and we're sitting at the big round table at Il Pirata. Il Pirata is an old family style Italian restaurant and bar located at the bottom of Potrero Hill. This isn't the Italian San Francisco that tourists know. This is not North Beach. Il Pirata sits amongst warehouses and industrial businesses. The red martini glass blinking outside the bar is the only light on the street at night. This is a restaurant for locals. My grandfather ate lunch at Il Pirata when he was a teamster. Il Pirata caters to the guys who move merchandise around the city and the men who load and unload the ships, the trucks and the freight trains. You can stop there on your way to and from the loading docks. "They make the biggest meatball sandwich in the city," my grandfather told me. He held out his huge hands about foot apart. "Like this," he said. "The size of a shoebox." All the food at Il Pirata is big food. The restaurant hasn't changed in thirty years.

Inside the restaurant, fake grape leaves and plastic grapes cover the walls and ceiling. Tall bottles of Chianti line the top of the lattice work. The backs of men hunker at the bar. They talk in whispers and coughs punctuated by the occasional yell and clap on the back. We're sitting at Pat's table. Pat is a 65 year old Sicilian. He's originally from Boston, but he's been in San Francisco for twenty years. Pat holds force at the table. He's the boss. The man. The big guy. Pat snaps his fingers and the waiter brings milk. He snaps his fingers and the waiter brings another glass of champagne. He snaps his fingers and stars shoot from his diamond studded fingers. His body is thick and solid as concrete. Under his handmade Italian suit, his skin is covered with scars from bullets and knives. Once Pat put my fingers on a crater carved deep into his chest. "Feel this," he told me. "There's a bullet wedged right next to my heart. If they took it out, it would kill me. The bullet grew a muscle around it. Now it's part of my body. I'll die with it inside me."

My grandfather is far away on the other side of the city, eating my grandmother's red sauce and playing his accordion. He has no idea his teenage granddaughter is sitting at the big round table at Il Pirata celebrating Vince's birthday. Vince is Pat's son. He wears his wife Chelsea on his arm like some kind of exotic collie. In fact, Chelsea looks a lot like a collie. Her hair explodes in giant tufts of red fur from her perfectly proportioned head. Chelsea obviously watched way too many Ann Margaret movies in her life, and she wears her red mane like some kind of proof of her worth. Her body is buried in piles of white mink, and her eyelashes are the length of crayons. She's so full of glitter and glamour that it's like someone cut her out of the movie screen and stuck her onto Vince's arm. Chelsea is big time. Everything about her is diamonds, gold, and money. She goes to Las Vegas, works the casinos and rakes in thousands in cash with her lithe red-haired Texan body. I am always stunned by Chelsea.

Me? I'm a sixteen-year-old girl who's barely grown tits. Pat took me in and made me his prize possession. I'm all decked out in a fox fur coat and silk dress. I feel ludicrously small inside these thousand dollar clothes. My body is used to blue jeans and cotton shirts. It never knew fur or silk before Pat. The whole table must be wearing a quarter million bucks in furs, diamonds, and designer clothes. We're like some kind of living wildlife museum with all these animal skins. The dresses and suits – Valentino, Anne Klein, Armani – are all stolen. We are some kind of high society in our clothes fresh from the boosters. You see, this is a gathering of a mob family – the low end of the mafia that deals in stolen goods and the sex trade. And I'm right there in the middle of it because I am a mob girl. I also happen to be Pat's hottest product of the moment because I am young and fresh. There is nothing old tired tricks want more than new young ass. I am that ass. When some old fucker rolls into town and wants his dick sucked or his ass whacked with a hairbrush or to be ridden like a horse while a girl howls like a dog, Pat sends me to the hotel. I am the girl, and I bring home the cash. In other words, Pat is my pimp, and I am his whore. And Pat makes sure my milk glass is full.

Pat's not the only pimp at the table. Big fat Dutch sits across from me bulging out of his Ultra Suede jacket. His neck is the size of an elephant leg. Pointed sideburns grow from his jowls like daggers. Dutch's huge face always shines like he coats it with Vaseline everyday. I'm scared that if I stare at it too hard, his whole head will pop and some kind of foul grease will erupt out of it. A giant gold horn charm dangles at Dutch's chest and points to his mountainous gut. He wears this horn like a gold cock, a testament to his masculinity. Really though, the gold horn is the Italian symbol for good luck. In fact everyone at the table is wearing a gold horn around their neck, even me. We are all in this life of crime together, and we need all the good luck we can get, even if our good luck was lifted from a downtown jewelry store. Dutch has two girls on each side, each one of them in full-length black mink. "My girls always wear mink," Dutch blows out a stream of cigar smoke and bad breath. The girls stare down at the table with empty eyes. Their eyelashes fall to their cheeks like black weeds. They are glazed and high and speechless. Dutch likes to keep his girls on dope.

The waiter brings giant platters of antipasti, and I immediately reach for the salami. I grab little rolled tubes of pink meat and gobble them down in a flash. I could live off salami. When I was a little girl, I would ride my bike to the deli every Saturday and buy 50 cents' worth of salami with my allowance. I would open the white paper, peel off a pink oval one slice at a time, and hold it up to the light. They sliced it so thin you could see right through it. I would stare at the rosy flesh, the little white circles of fat, and then slip the slice into my mouth. It tasted like heaven.

Pat's wife Lulu sits on the other side of Pat. Even if I am Pat's current prize possession, Lulu will always be his number one whore and his number one love. Lulu has a heart of gold to go with the horn she wears around her neck. She watches me devour the salami and wash it down with milk. "Slow down," she laughs. "You don't want to get sick before your dinner gets here."

Dinner isn't going to get here for a while. Il Pirata is an old family-style Italian restaurant, so before the main course comes, we have to eat our way through antipasti, minestrone, bread, and tortellini. When my main course does come, there is no doubt what it will be. Veal scaloppini. I always order the veal scaloppini because veal scaloppini is the most special thing on the menu. I know this because veal scaloppini was the most special thing we ate at home or at my grandmother's house. When my mom or grandmother made veal, it was a really big deal. Veal is very expensive. You have to kill little baby cows to get the veal. A baby cow doesn't have anywhere near the meat you get from a big grown-up cow. It takes a lot of baby cows to make a lot of veal. "The little baby cows have to be fed milk," my grandmother always said. "Or the meat is no good. The milk-fed veal is the good veal. If it's not milk-fed, then it's tough and stringy, like chewing on an old shoe."

Then my grandmother would tell me how to prepare the veal just right. She picked up a little metal hammer covered with sharp points. "You have to pound the flesh gently like this," my grandmother said as she started pounding the pink meat with the hammer. "If you pound the veal just right, it's so tender it will melt in your mouth."

Every time my grandmother cooked veal, my grandfather asked if it was milk-fed. "Is that milk-fed?" he asked from his place at the table. My grandmother stopped what she was doing, lit a cigarette and blew a stream of smoke into my grandfather's face. She shook her head and went back to pounding the veal.

I suck down the last of my milk before diving into the tortellini. Little round rings of pasta stuffed with cheese. Pat stabs a little pasta pillow with his fork and holds it up. "See this," he says. "You know it's a good tortellini if it looks like a cunt. And you know it's a good cunt if it looks like tortellini." He puts it in his mouth and swallows it.

Chelsea holds out her hand and wags a giant red ruby under Pat's nose. "Did you see what Vincent got me?" she asks. Pat puts on his reading glasses, pulls Chelsea's hand to his face and studies the ring.

"Nice stone," he says and raises his eyebrows to Vince. Vince shrugs his shoulders, reaches over and opens Chelsea's coat. Underneath her coat, Chelsea is wearing a shiny gold halter dress. Her breasts bulge out of the sides like perfectly smooth white balls. They're so round they look like they're going to roll right off her. Vince puts one hand on each breast and squeezes. "And how about these?"

For the next few minutes Chelsea talks about her new boob job and all the money she made in Vegas over the weekend. "You should see her," Vince says. "She walks in there, and everyone thinks she's a movie star."

I think about the photograph of my father on my grandmother's kitchen counter, his bald head glowing under the casino lights at the Golden Nugget. He lives in Las Vegas and sends my grandmother an endless supply of poker cards. I wonder if he's seen Chelsea in Vegas, if he thinks she's a movie star, if he's fucked her.

I'm starting on the minestrone now and fishing out kidney beans. Vince is talking about a load of stereos that just came in and how he needs to off them. Al is here. He owns a chain of dirty bookstores and sex shops in the Tenderloin and on Polk Street. Al says he can help unload the stereos if he can get a cut. Pat tells Vince to let Al help him. Vince tells Al he'll give him a cut. The deal is done. I'm soaking up broth with bread and thinking about the brand new microwave oven in my grandmother's kitchen. The brand new stereo that plays her favorite Harry Belafonte albums. The brand new television sets in every room of her house. All gifts my father sends her from Las Vegas. I wonder if my father could help Vince unload the stereos.

I pick up my empty milk glass and scrape the straw in the edges trying to catch the last drops. The straw makes a loud gurgling sound, and Pat reaches over and slaps my hand from the glass. He snaps his fingers and tells the waiter to give me more milk.

"Don't you think you're too old to be drinking milk, honey?" Chelsea asks me. Her teeth are stacked like ivory tiles between her lips.

"I like milk," I say as the waiter puts a full glass of milk and a giant plate of veal scaloppini in front of me.

"You keep eating like that and your ass is going to get so fat no one's going to pay five dollars for it," Chelsea laughs and picks at an olive rolling around on her plate.

"Her ass is just fine," Pat says. He grabs my butt and pinches it with all his force. I feel two fat bruises swell on my left ass cheek.

I stab a piece of veal with my fork and slide it between my lips. The calf meat is so delicious it feels like it's melting on my tongue. I close my eyes and feel it slip down my throat. Soft, tender, milk-fed.

"When are you going to get her a mink coat?" Chelsea looks me up and down.

"She doesn't need a mink coat to be a beauty." Pat puts his arm around me and gives me a squeeze. "Do you, baby?"

Chelsea's mouth pulls into a frown. Lines open up like fissures under her eyes and around her lips. I stare at her lips and feel like I'm going to fall inside them.

I remember the one time I turned a trick with Chelsea. His name was Bill, and he was one of her old tricks she'd known for years. Bill opened the door to his hotel room, and the smell of vodka, sweat and cigar stuck its fat fingers down my throat and made me retch. Bill was a rough pot-bellied man, and he was drunk as a dog. According to Chelsea, Bill was a millionaire. Millionaire or not, he was ugly and stunk like bar, piss and a thousand stale cigars.

"Bill, baby!" Chelsea squealed in her high-pitched Texas drawl. She pulled his cigar out of his mouth and planted her perfect plum lips on his. "We're going to have us some fun tonight," she oozed.

Chelsea waved her hand at me to come closer to her and Bill. "Don't be afraid, darling. Bill's not going to bite you. Now come in here and help me wash up this poor man."

Chelsea led me and Bill into the bathroom and handed me a washcloth and bar of soap. I stood there soaping up Bill's dick. I slathered the flaccid thing with soap and water. It flopped against his leg. Bill grabbed his pathetic prick and gave it a tug. "Do it harder," he mumbled through his cigar. Bill was too drunk to get it up.

"Don't you worry about that, baby," Chelsea crooned. "We'll take care of you."

The rest of the night went something like this. Bill's dead fish dick was in my mouth and I tried not to puke from the smell of sweat on his balls. Then Bill's dick was in Chelsea's mouth and she didn't seem to smell anything. Bill's big hand pulled me to his face and made me kiss him. His tongue was thick as a piece of liver, and his breath rancid with cigar and vodka. His face was so rough with whiskers, I figured my face would be in shreds when I was done and I'd be wearing band-aids on it for weeks. Bill's breath was the worst breath I ever tasted and smelled in my life. Even after he took his tongue out of my mouth, I could feel the weight of it and taste the slimy sick coat it left inside me. And there was Chelsea's perfectly glamorous body. There was Chelsea glittering like the Hope Diamond as she opened her perfectly rosy lips and swallowed Bill's lifeless prick. She was real Las Vegas big time in this hotel room with Bill's dick in her mouth.

Bill's dead fish still wasn't doing anything, and we needed to get out of there. Chelsea reached in her bag and grabbed a bottle of lube. She squirted a little pool in her palm and jerked on Bill's dick while he pinched my nipples until they felt like they were falling off. Finally Chelsea climbed on top of Bill, bounced up and down a few times, and tossed her giant mane of red hair in violent circles. Bill let out a heave and a grunt. Chelsea rolled off him. "You're so hot, baby. How do you know how to do that to me?" Bill picked up the stub of his cigar and flipped the television on with the remote control.

Chelsea got up and padded to the bathroom. I sat on a chair and watched the light from the bathroom spill across the hotel room floor. Chelsea's naked body was framed by the bathroom door. She climbed onto the sink and squatted over the faucet. She slapped water onto her cunt over and over with a slapping sloshing sound, her bare ass hanging over the edge of the sink. "You going to come wash up?" she asked me.

I was frozen. Watching Chelsea on her haunches in the bathroom sink was even more shocking than the image of Chelsea's pink Texas lips wrapped around Bill's limp dick. "When you're done," I said.

And now here's Chelsea sitting across from me with her white mink, her giant ruby ring, her new boobs, and her pimento-stuffed olive rolling around on her plate. "I need to go powder my nose," Chelsea breathes across the table. She leans over to Vince and kisses him, one eye glaring at me while her little pink tongue shoots into Vince's mouth.

"I can never be like Chelsea!" I cry to Pat when Chelsea is gone.

"Don't you worry about her, baby," Pat tells me. "You don't need to be like Chelsea. You've got your youth. Your youth is worth a thousand mink coats."

I look at my freshly filled glass of milk, pull out the red plastic straw, and guzzle it down straight from the glass. Milk dries and cakes around my lips, but I don't wipe it off.

Chelsea sits back down at the table and goes back to poking at her olive. I stab a hunk of veal with my fork and hold it to my lips. I smile at Chelsea and feel the milk crack on my face. Then I slide the veal inside my mouth and start chewing.

"How's the veal tonight?" Dutch asks me.

"Perfect," I say and swallow another piece.

SON OF A LEMON
Nick Matros
(with apologies to Eugenio Montale)

Ascoltami, i poeti italo-americani
si muovono soltanto fra gli antenati
nonni, bisnonni, e zii di zii.

Listen to me, Italian-American poets
Move only among the ancestors
Nonna, nonno, zii di zii.
I, rather, love tree-lined sidewalks
Cracked and distorted from uprooting,
Used as ramps for kids on bikes,
Reminding me of Massapequa streets,
Where, Sundays, I did the same
On rides around my grandparents' house
Whom I never called Nonno or Nonna

Better not to quote the rare phrase of dialect
That proves to doubters that I'm of their origin,
Although my last name ends not in a vowel.
Aunt Carmela married Uncle Sam, a Polish Jew
Who served and survived at D-Day,
Though his name changed the vowel from A to Y,
Thus changing their ethnicity and
Perhaps explaining their excess of decoration at Xmas.
Similarly, Mom married a Russian whose last name sounds Greek,
At least, I still get to be Mediterranean.

We search for these traces of traditions that disappear
And meld over the past hundred years and hold them up
To claim, lie, insist, that this is who we still are
We've not been erased in assimilation
Although Giovanni married a Methodist,
And Joey, an Episcopalian.

We still eat *zeppole* at the feast
And stick a reflective tri-colore on our bumper
In celebration of all that made us risk our lives,
Divide our families, and escape in the first place
Once upon a time, to America.

We can't all keep our vowels unchanged,
We can't all still make it to Sunday dinner,
Though my Irish wife makes the sauce just like
Grandma, and neither she, nor Grandma, has
Called or will call it "Gravy"
Yes, *un 'irlandese* can cook like *una barese*
Cause it's a tradition we maintain without
Going to mass, hiding our minds, or staying in the neighborhood

Today she's making mussels, white sauce.

With a running start, I leap off the cracked, raised sidewalk
Avoiding the ever-growing roots that would otherwise trip me
And make my way at three in the morning to the Korean bodega
To buy myself, what in this country must pass,
As a lemon.

HUNGER
Gil Fagiani

Hunger
shadowed the hilltop towns
of Sicily after the war.

When the packet arrived Christmas week
the Giacomelli family of ten
blessed their relatives in America
for their kindness, *generosità*.

With fumbling fingers
they peeled off the brown packing,
removed coffee, sugar, cornmeal, flour
and a glass jar filled with gray powder.

That week much bread,
cake and coffee were consumed
and when nothing was left but the jar
92-year-old Attilio Giacomelli
mixed the powder with milk, ate it as porridge.

Not long after New Years the letter arrived
from Ninfa, Attilio's niece
telling him of his brother Giovanni's death
and his wish to have the ashes
scattered across the land where he was born.

A HARMFUL YET FUNNY AND SOMEWHAT HONESTLY TRUTHFUL STEREOTYPE
Michael Carosone

"I can't be Italian anymore,"
she screamed,
from the kitchen
as she was stuffing
her face
with fresh mozzarella,
tomato, and basil
over Italian bread
soaked in olive oil and garlic,
"It is too fattening,"
to her husband,
sitting on his recliner
in the living room,
watching the Yankees
beat the shit out of the Mets
in one of his
pleasurable subway series,
as he sat behind
the fake wooden snack table,
eating a huge bowl of spaghetti,
maybe marinara,
maybe meatballs,
sausage, pork,
with a nice cold antipasto,
drinking a fine chianti,
not listening to a word she says,
or screams,
across the rooms,
in their 84th Street
Bensonhurst   Brooklyn
New York City   New York State
Italian-America apartment.

WRITING HISTORY
Amy Barone

Did it begin in Italy in the shadow of La Maiella where a young man
    trudged down unpaved roads in search of a better life, a bigger world,
    new prospects for love and work
Leaving behind brothers and sisters with whom he'd never again share
    a meal or a laugh or a hug
Resolved to set stakes in an unseen land and never look back

How does New York fit in where a mismatched couple met and married
    at Our Lady of Mount Carmel Church
An unassuming truck driver with his driven wife who taught English to
    immigrant children while raising eight offspring
East Harlem residents for years until they were enticed away to a street
    of row homes filled with paesani

Or are the true origins Pennsylvania where another mismatched couple
    met and married
An ambitious hardware merchant with his English teacher wife who quit
    work to raise three daughters
Depression-era parents who knew how to stretch a dime, worked hard
    at everything, instilled values and morals, but found time for travel and play

Why the lure to Italy? To know them better, to learn their language, to
    walk the roads now paved
Where the secrets unraveled of how to be an Italian, how to be an American
And you couldn't stay forever as hard as you tried – like them, always
    looking ahead to new opportunities

Have you now come full circle, dropping anchor in New York, a place
    that overwhelmed you as a child
Inhabiting a multicultural universe where no one invites you over for an
    espresso or suggests a lake ride on a quiet Sunday afternoon
Where you struggle like those who came before, but no paesano holds
    out a hand

NONNO
Cameron McHenry

"Oh shit yeah, goddamn right, *che cazzo* what a good time,
good taste, good life."
Nonno, grandfather, you have the crudest lust,
the type that rears from the gut
and forces everything around you into the splendor of performance.

For years I'd never seen that oak tree in front of the old lodge,
but you reacted to its knots and gnarled leaves
as though it'd been erected on the stage of Carnegie Hall
to shudder faintly in the butterfly light.

Food tastes better when you're near me,
the orphan in you learned at a young age to savor
every spoonful of broth the matrons boiled
in the back of your cold classroom.
Even now you act astonished that pizza exists,
ranting on at length about the exquisite flavor of cheese,
the twisting spice of tomato sauce, the snap of crust,
and hearty swallow.

I often wonder how you lived through
your first taste of Nonna's cooking?
After all these years fireworks still blow out of your mouth
every time she enters the room, a slather of slap happy vulgarity
that insults her churchliness and makes her blush,
your Italian Bride, who quietly beams when you spotlight
the lushness of her legs, the exquisiteness of her antipasta,
the history of her Lucchese upbringing.

You never knew your lineage,
but the day you married Flora you started speaking Italian.
Now you are more Italian than any of us,

telling intimate stories about how you and Mario got drunk on Grappa
and spent the night running into olive trees all over Lucca.
You always drink too much wine, eat too much, swear too much,
and sometimes cry

but at the end of the night in the midst of goodbyes you only say,
"ti voglio bene, ci vediamo presto presto!" and hold me so tightly
I can feel your heart beating the bloodline that binds us.
You are an orphan holding your granddaughter,
we both understand this.

Last week you had open-heart surgery,
a new heart for you birthday, you said.
When the doctors cracked open your chest,
I imagine that wine bottles and love poetry sprang out
like figures in a pop-up card.

They fixed what they could,
and somehow sewed all that life force back inside you.
Now you just need to live, *Nonno, devi soltanto vivere.*
The best in all of us, the lusty, indulgent, mighty light in all of us,
the Italian that rages in all of us
needs you to rise and say:
"Oh shit yeah, goddamn right, *che cazzo* what a good time,
good taste, good life!"

PAPERS
Jim Provenzano

Clouds bleed away to strands, shredded by the bumpy Tuscan hills. It's usually quieter up here, but even down in the village it's the pause before supper, é la sosta della cena, to paraphrase a poet who got his skull crushed.

But that was a long time ago. They don't do that here anymore.

I put the champagne in the tub filled with precious ghiaccio. Three things I brought for the final return; an ice machine, screens for the windows, and sponge mops.

There are some things you miss. In the midst of beautiful biscotti, I crave messy oatmeal cookies. We get all the music. TV is a hoot. I Simpson! But these are trifles. I think of the big joys, the joy of escape, of truth, the pleasure of picking away at the lies. American ones, that is.

If #3 applies to you, you must obtain your paternal grandfather's birth certificate from Italy

Was it a pay-off, perhaps? The brother who never left here. It could happen. Was he like me? Would they have let him out? Or something else completely. What if he was a criminal? Wasn't I one, once? Well, illegal in half the country. But not here. Here, I am Seniore Finocchio. Here, I am legal in every province, sexually and residentially. And I can prove it.

his marriage certificate (certified copy with "apostille," and all of the documents listed for #1, except for your father's naturalization certificate,

There are echoes after trying to get something from Dad like the truth, like memories, if any. They come in echoes like long-distance carriers that don't work. I wanted to know what happened to his unmarried uncle, the one who never left. Dad couldn't remember that.

because in this case you will need your paternal grandfather's naturalization papers, showing that he was naturalized after your father's birth,

I would have stayed, for the weather, or my apartment, or healthcare. Except there's a river an hour's hike from here, and you can't do flip turns in the river, that's for sure, but it's beautiful. It works. If you want a pool you have to take the bus into Cascina. If you want the beach, Livorno's half an hour past that. Of course it's cruisy. Italy has such lovely statues. And they go out walking at night.

Wilde said it better.

No, I don't drive. Without trains, I would never meet such men. Italian men, are cautious, delicate, so wounded some of them, while others just have all the charm in the world. They flirt, sure, and no, they don't all... No, it's more of a thing here, where it's woven into conversation, all of it, the church, sex, mortality, mushrooms, sauce. I mean, it's not like in San Francisco, or New York, where you have your Health Space and your Drink Space and your Sex Space, and it's all ....

Forget it. I'm not getting into that cross-cultural dialectic.

They are not how you see them. How I saw them. Here, men kiss me goodbye and hello with more affection than lovers of that place, what I/we/they once called Mecca. Here no one forgets me after meeting. Here nobody asks how to spell my name.

My family. Where is my family? Can you tell me that? Is it here on this map? In this flag?

It is only with a sense of removal that one can identify a situation. From here, the trajectory of critique gathers oceanic momentum. They call me an expatriate, patriot, qualunque.

"The greatest patriotism is to tell your country when it is behaving dishonorably, foolishly, viciously." Barnes said that, way before the 700 Club became the Seven-Headed Beast Club. No, Barnes didn't say that here. I'm just quoting him. I don't even know the guy. Well, yes, we do get celebrities here, but not the English kind.

Every time I go into town, I see grandpa's brother's grandson, or me, or a beautiful cousin to kiss hello. The entire countryside is ripe with incestuous possibilities. Dad always said Caribinieri with affection. Now I see why; uniforms, blue as the Florentine sky on a primavera pastorale.

Dad had to be reminded four times to please send the papers, or just copies. I really had a chance, even without Marisa, the Roman dyke who bowed out at the last minute. She eventually "came to an impasse on the inner political ramifications of mimicking the patriarchy." Marisa, the Roman who studied in Bologna.

That joke doesn't translate.

At the last job I had in America, every day, coming back from lunch, I passed a bank. In the window a sign tempted me like pastry: Foreign Currency.

I remember days when I thought I'd finished my research. Well, let's just say, held off. The papers, the papers. Immigrants to Canada. Italian immigrants in Peoria, Jewish Italian immigration and elements of racist pre-war policies, (Fintzi-Continis, Garden of, see also).

Now I mail them around to go to *i conferenzi di lettere.* That's where you meet all the cute and smart guys.

or a statement from U.S. Immigration in Washington D.C. and from the Court of the County in which he resided stating that according to their records he was

Take for example, Massimo. He's coming tonight. He's this guy, whoever he is, who is everything that came before him. And since he's gay, it's like, we're both the end of the line, unless we have kids, which maybe he could have. I wondered this as I kissed him good afternoon from a bathhouse shower stall (where we met), or on a field (where we met again) and I wanted to play "find the coachman" from A Room With a View and dump all those stuffy Brits off to the side of the road.

This is where it happens. Where I see Anthony and Sebastian and Joseph and everybody, teary-eyed, religious epiphanies and sexual heat. The banal dailiness glorified by familiarity and exoticism. Green Jesuses on Byzantine frescoes, the skin tone two hundred-year-old mildew. Smells so heavy they change your body composition.

Feel of Ellis Island, Need for at least an uncle or Somebody nearby to pick on, be Joked with, Loved no matter what, Remembered for everything you say, Dear loved one, Before you go, Take this...

You must also submit a "certified copy" bearing the "apostille" or your claim will be refused (or, if in fact he was naturalized before your father's birth then neither you nor your father qualify for Italian citizenship under category # 3).

In Milan, the second visit, I had lunch with the British editor of L'Uomo Vogue, who took me to the Duomo, and the big old mall beside it. He was happy that I'd remembered him. I was happy to see him still employed. Versace models sauntered by, simply going to work. I spoke of residency. He offered to make arrangements.

I'm glad I studied my Italian, which of course he refuses to speak, saying things in more poetic ways than my too many words do, you know? Such *melancolia con energia, cosa una latte.* He'll be down next month to visit. The owners don't mind. As long as I take care of the place, it's fine. No, we don't date. That would be absurd.

A travel agent in Florence once filled a plastic bag full of tourist maps, booklets, pamphlets, hotels brochures, all about Calabria. On impulse, I had decided to go south. I wanted to find the documents for myself.

I looked at the brochures. The pictures of "resorts" resembled Pennsylvania off-road motor lodges. Here you have your Best Western *con mini-bar, ma sensa bagno. Doccia, si, ma non ho bagno.* Here you have your gay peasant dances.

I told the travel lady, who had finished unloading my now four pounds of brochures and was on the phone with Alitalia, that I was hoping to live in Italy someday.

She said, "Whatever for?"

To find my roots? Dietary restrictions? Because my country is decaying less elegantly than yours? Because it's best to avoid large groupings of fervently religious people at the shift of any millennium, and what safer place than Italy?

At L'Uficia de la Comune di Cairoli, I became a regular to them. I visited their offices, every day for a week, searching files, being allowed one ledger at a time, repeatedly stepping to the copy machine, inserting lire coins, blinding the decaying pages, repeating the gesture with the solemnity of a monk.

We raise a glass to friends gone, except those who live. The others will be remembered, those who survived the last years of la secola in the country that failed to live up to its beautiful Italian name.

È strano, the circularity of events. Where once the boot trampled, now it digs flower beds. Lucky, the foresight of those who know how to fill out forms.

My English, it curls and flakes like ancient faxes.

FIORI DA MORTI
Tommi Avicolli Mecca

Papa
who worked with your brother 50 years
at that Sunoco station in South Philly
holding court to a group of retired men who called
you Teenaxe

Papa
who gave me change to buy comic books
from the old man at the corner newsstand who
called me Tony, which was your name

Papa
who gave me my first job wiping windshields
I could barely reach on my tippy-toes
sometimes you held me up or I stood on a wooden box
to reach the glass

Papa
who decided I was gonna be a priest
bragging to all your friends when I became an altar boy
prouder still when your brother nicknamed me
"the little father"

Papa
who won me a pink elephant at the Steel Pier in Atlantic City
you called him "Lucky"
I hugged him all the way home
afraid he might disappear

Papa
who was never lucky at anything
especially politics

wanting to be more than a neighborhood committeeman
but knocked down every time you tried

Papa
who watched helplessly as I divorced your world
going to anti-war rallies
growing my hair, listening to rock music
even tasting a boy's lips on mine
I became the enemy you ranted about every night
sitting at the dinner table watching the news

Papa
who cursed me
when I came out at Temple University
my picture on the front page of the student paper
my face on your TV
your worst nightmare

Papa
who asked me to change my name
so I wouldn't embarrass la famiglia

Papa
who threw me out of the house when I was 19

Papa
who screamed, "You're not my son"

Papa
who cried when I yelled back, "I don't wanna be your son"

Papa
you're gone now
& all those angry words still haunt me
we never took them back

PICCOLA ITALIA
George Guida

When the last italoparlante expires,
we'll finally open our business,
the Vegas idea, casino-culture spa,
Piccola Italia.

Guests will arrive with coupons
we mass mail in October,
redeemable for plastic chips and a lesson
in present-tense Italian verbs,

because italianitá is a gamble,
which comes from living the tongue.
They'll have to learn at least,
"Dov'é la mia camera?" before check-in.

Campanile bells of Norman design
will clang us all awake, three hours before work
for espressi and biscotti
from a dead nonna's recipe.

Guests, called cittadini,
will walk to Il Centro Storico
to work with actors trained
on weeks of Rai Uno tapes.

On the way we'll force them to chat
with paesani re-enactors
in streets the width of a fiat,
copied from a town outside Naples.

Many will apprentice to masons
at work on a massive cathedral

where the Bishop of Nevada will say mass
to a handful of make-believe goomads.

One week in we'll simulate steerage.
Contadini/guests will journey to a dock
on our Atlantic lagoon, where they'll sleep
with bedrolls and children we supply.

They'll spend three nights aboard our steamer,
La Stella Meridionale, below,
in a dark room filled with cow manure
chemically treated to smell like human waste.

Off the boat they'll disperse,
led by padroni played by croupiers,
settle in different hotel blocks
organized by villages we assign.

After two more weeks of labor,
when they can speak Italian well enough to joke,
we'll help them, day by day, to forget,
so they have to remember

the culture now in their bones
until the day they earn enough chips
from work and the slots, to cash out
for the suburbs that are their destiny.

THE IMPENETRABLE CROSSING
Giancarlo Campagna

In the shelter of each other the people live. —Anonymous

Women come out with their boxes emptying the houses
of children and small bags.

They are strong to live on embers,
take the bricks out of dams
to let the waters flow.

A dream behind the dream
that exists behind the words
of those at watch at the gates.

They've dreamed the lion to enter
the forest where the cover is for them
a kind of charity.

They'll travel with their canes
and their bushels, and with dogs
tumbling after them heavy with dust.

The sea will be a distant longing.
The sky will bide above the boughs.
To them the walking will be sufficient
as they know there are no borders
amidst the trees.

The shade will be enough.
And so will the cool waters.

Setting their packs down will be a gift.
And to ease their muscles will come to them like song.

Dances will spontaneously sprout along some creek bed.
Slugs or small snakes turned out of the sand will be held
over a flame.

Whatever's eaten will be a suicide.

And they'll dance far longer than
The music can make its melodies.

So much will be forgotten in the sleep of the gullies.

The world will turn and the people will grow young again.
And the children will hurry before them and announce
the discoveries of new trails or caves or large silent birds with colorful plumes
or the great wisps of spider webs holding the carcasses of eagles.

And they'll continue to walk
And forget their lives.

Some will rename their children after exposed roots or minerals.
Some will collect stones and keep them around their necks with old fishing nets.

Almost everything of their former lives will be forgotten.

And they will smile in the mornings after the morning fire
And watch their skin grow luminescent.

COLUMBUS, THE MAFIA & DENIAL
Ed Coletti

In fourteen hundred ninety-two
Columbus sailed the Ocean blue.

1.
Columbus Circle   June 29th 1971
Joe Columbo   shot into 7-year coma
not by Laughing Otter
nor by Green Rock Woman
not even Crazy Horse
or Crazy Joe Gallo
but by an African-American
Jerome Johnson.
It was about Columbo's thing
not our thing
as in my thing
but Cosa Nostra as in
Mafia's Thing as in
Christopher Columbus's
thing, that made-man who
dwells among us ever since.

Joe Columbo   only 40
youngest mob boss ever
maintained to the press
"There ain't no mafia, no cosa nostra!"
And that Christopher Columbus
was a "great Italian role model."
Today we might call him
A made-man
by those Cappi di Tutti Cappi
somehow Spanish
Cabezas de Todas Cabezas
Jefes de Todos Jefes

who kissed Cristobal
on each Italian cheek
The naming is the creation:
"Let there be Cristobal Colon
from Cristoforo Colombo,
And there was.
Hence forth this Made-Man
to make our History!

2.
Indians! Indians! Columbus cried;
His heart was filled with joyful pride.

Columbus announced,
"When you ask for something they have,
They never say no.
Give me, give me Gold, Gold, Gold!
Give me, give me Slave, Slave, Slave!"
And I seriously doubt he ever said,
"Please."

3.
He made the trip again and again,
Trading gold to bring to Spain.

Joe Columbo and the Gambino gang
Traded in heroin all over Harlem.
They didn't bring it to a king or president.
They just brought it along with
Protection, prostitutes, and numbers rackets.
"There ain't no mafia, no cosa nostra,"
Columbo cried, but La Cosa Nostra
Sails on and on like those
Three little ships... (that) left from Spain
(Columbus, this poor excuse for an Italian)
Sailed through sunshine, wind, and rain.